GUIDEPOSTS
FOR GROWING UP

GUIDEPOSTS FOR GROWING UP

by BARBARA K. POLLAND, *Ph.D.*

STANDARD EDUCATIONAL CORPORATION
Chicago 1993

Barbara K. Polland holds a Ph.D. in Human Development from Clare-
mont Graduate School of Education, an M.A. in Guidance and Counseling from San Fernando Valley State College, and a B.Ed. in Elementary
Education from National College of Education. She is also a licensed
Marriage, Family, and Child Therapist. She holds the position of profes-
sor of child development at California State University, Northridge, and
is also a therapist in private practice, working with children with varied
backgrounds and needs.

Dr. Polland is a member of the National Association for the Education
of Young Children, the Association for Childhood Education Interna-
tional, the California Association of Marriage and Family Therapists, and
the Free Arts Clinic for Abused Children. She is the author of *Grandma
and Grampa Are Special People; Decisions, Decisions, Decisions; Feelings:
Inside You and Outloud Too;* and *The Sensible Book: A Celebration of Your
Five Senses.* Dr. Polland is the mother of two children.

Library of Congress Cataloging-in-Publication Data

Polland, Barbara K., 1939–
    Guideposts for growing up / by Barbara K. Polland.
      p.   cm.—(Child horizons)
    Includes index.
    ISBN 0-87392-208-5
    1. Child development.   2. Child rearing.   3. Child psychology.
    I. Title
    HQ767.9.P65   1991
    649'.1—dc20   91-20391
                                                              CIP

Printed and Manufactured in the United States of America

Dedication

This book is dedicated to
parents and children learning
to celebrate their
shared experience.

Contents

ACKNOWLEDGMENTS

Love to my children, Tamy and Mark, who continually challenge me to find effective approaches to parenting.

Respect and admiration to Dr. John I. Goodlad. Thank you for suggesting my name and believing that I could write this book.

To my dear friend Connie Tunick, whose continued support and encouragement helped every step of the way.

To the California State University, Northridge, Research Team whose readings and discussions helped launch this book: Jeff McKenzie, Ellie Rabkin, Geni Torsney, Stacy Borock, Olga Koonin, and Margaret Ladany.

My appreciation to students, therapy clients, and parent groups for sharing and raising many of the concerns used in this book.

—Barbara K. Polland
Los Angeles

INTRODUCTION

Being a parent requires no classes, academic degrees, or licenses. Children do not arrive with a set of instructions or a manual, and parents often have to learn as they go, receiving "on-the-job training." Being a parent is a complicated job, and no amount of reading can completely prepare parents for all the experiences that they may encounter. But, although some experiences may be unique to particular families, there are certain similarities that all families share. Families that seem very different may be very much alike when it comes to the demands of child rearing and the questions and concerns that parents have. It can be helpful for parents to remember that they are not alone. Because most parents are concerned with becoming more effective, this book explores solutions to the problems parents typically face at various stages in their children's lives, using a question-and-answer format.

The way in which our parents raised us generally has a dramatic effect on the way we choose to raise our children. As parents, we should make an effort to recall specific events from childhood. By thinking about how things were handled in our families as we were growing up, we can gain new insights into ourselves as parents. We can then decide what we would like to duplicate and what we would like to do differently in raising our own children.

During the early years, children are totally dependent on their parents for food, protection, shelter, and physical care. Children also need social and moral guidance. The family unit is critically important because the stability that it provides helps children to acquire independence. When members of a family are able to rely on one another, interdependence occurs. Parents need to provide a framework in which children can learn to be gradually more independent and eventually able to manage their own lives and live on their own.

There are no "perfect parents" or "perfect children." When we recognize our own shortcomings and strengths, we become more accepting of our children. It is then easier to accept our children for themselves, rather than trying to make them into what we wish they would be.

How children feel about themselves depends largely on how their parents feel about them. Many children feel inadequate because they are never quite able to meet their parents' expectations. It is so frustrating to fail continually that some children decide to give up the struggle. Such children might become passive, depressed, and uninterested in life. Or their repressed feelings could turn to anger, making them aggressive enough to be a danger to society. When parents contribute to a child's negative self-image, unwanted feelings and behavior are only perpetuated. Parents must do all they can to encourage children to feel good about themselves. When a child feels important in his or her parents' eyes, each day can be faced with self-confidence.

Parents have daily opportunities to show their love for their children, and they face daily decisions about setting limits for them. Giving love and setting limits are essential parts of being parents. Parents who abdicate the latter responsibility are not doing their children a favor. Without limits, children can become overindulged and out of control and may seem anxious, fearful, or just plain obnoxious. When parents provide firm guidance, children know their boundaries and feel more confident about parental expectations.

Children need rules, but they do not always agree with them. Such conflict is an inevitable part of living together and growing as a family. When treated respectfully, children are more likely to accept their parents' suggestions and rules. But being a successful parent does not mean avoiding all disagreements. Instead, parents should focus on resolving conflicts constructively. This approach to problem solving can improve family relationships and can be a learning experience for everyone involved.

Guideposts for Growing Up suggests ways in which parents can help children solve problems while enhancing their feelings of self-worth. Each section of the book attempts to help parents appreciate the developmental hurdles that children must face. Because children change dramatically as they grow, families need to be prepared for new developments. Most problems have many possible solutions, and no single method of problem solving works all the time. One rigid set of rules could not possibly be appropriate for every family, because human interactions do not follow such rules. It can be helpful, however, to have certain guidelines to follow. This book offers such guidelines to help its readers improve their skills as parents.

Most of the problems discussed in this book are age related. It is important to remember that behavior that is normal for a child of one age may be highly abnormal for an older or younger child. However, when considering a description of the typical behavior for children of a certain age, parents must allow for individual differences, as there are always exceptions.

Parents need not become anxious that their child is "slow" or has problems when their expectations for his or her age level are not met. Two children of the same age may well behave differently. Each child has a unique growth pattern, and variations in growth rarely give cause for alarm. For example, Johnny might be adept at throwing a ball, while Jimmy, who is the same age, fumbles just trying to pick one up. On the other hand, Jimmy's vocabulary might be more advanced than Johnny's.

This book asks that parents recognize and appreciate their children's positive traits and skills. Sometimes it is easy to become preoccupied with problems and forget our children's accomplishments. The book offers help and encouragement for the more difficult, but typical, conflicts, which can sometimes seem overwhelming.

Daily routines help children to feel safe by making life predictable. Parents need to provide this stability. But once routines have been established, slight changes can turn an everyday event into an adventurous, fun-filled experience. Risk trying some of the new approaches presented in this book even if you are a bit skeptical—they may prove rewarding. Some sections in the book might help you solve an immediate problem, and others might prepare you for a future challenge. *Guideposts for Growing Up* presents an optimistic approach to parenthood, one that encourages mutual respect, commitment, and love.

GUIDEPOSTS FOR GROWING UP

CHAPTER 1

HELPING CHILDREN TAKE CARE OF THEIR BODIES

This chapter is concerned with many day-to-day events in the lives of families. Included are sections on sleeptime, eating, clothing, and the bathroom. The way we handle these routines communicates to our children the importance we attach to bodily care. A positive approach on our part will lay the foundation for helping children deal successfully with medical environments, sexuality, and self-protection. These important topics are discussed in the concluding sections of this chapter.

As you read the concerns of other parents, you might identify with some, consider others past history, or recall similar incidents from your own childhood. The suggestions will help you to understand the philosophy of this chapter, which is based on the premise that it is an important function of parents to help their children take care of their own bodies.

SLEEPTIME

If everyone went to sleep at the same time, perhaps there would be fewer protests from children about ending their day. However, children know that the world goes right on being exciting and interesting long after they are asleep. Many children participate in power struggles with their parents to avoid going to sleep. This results in a negative closing to the day and parents losing time they need by themselves. Since it is impossible to make another person fall asleep, it is important to search for ways to calmly set the stage for sleep.

Preparing for Bed

Our two-and-a-half-year-old daughter is great about her afternoon nap and a pleasure to be with all day. But at bedtime she seems to get a second wind and she doesn't feel tired. My husband feels I should force her to go to sleep by shutting her door and letting her cry it out. I don't want to see the day end with tears.

There are a number of alternatives to having your daughter "cry it out." Perhaps her afternoon nap could be shortened. This will help her to be tired at bedtime. Also, begin to work out bedtime rituals that will provide your daughter with the same comfortable routine every night. A calming book, a record, or a back rub might help. Some children become relaxed after a warm bath or a glass of warm milk. If you are firm but loving about bedtime when your daughter is this young, you will set the stage for struggle-free bedtimes in the future.

Bedtime Rocking and Banging

My boys share a room, and the five-year-old has trouble falling asleep at night because his three-year-old brother rocks the crib as he bangs his head against the end of it. I tried keeping the older one up later and that helped. However, the little one wakes his brother by banging and rocking in the middle of the night. Is there something wrong with my son? He doesn't give me any other problems and seems fine in every other way, but now I'm starting to worry.

Head banging and crib rocking are done by perfectly normal children, who usually grow out of it during their third or fourth year. The rocking, banging motion probably sets the stage for their relaxing enough to fall asleep.

There are a few things you might want to try to help your five-year-old have an easier time sleeping. Your idea of staggering bedtimes is wise. Not only will your five-year-old avoid having to listen to his brother's bedtime noises, but he will have some time alone with you. To help older brother sleep when the three-year-old does his banging and rocking in the middle of the night, you can try putting a sound-absorbing mat underneath the crib and adding pads to the sides.

My daughter is eight and a delightful person until it is time to go to sleep. She calls to my wife or me at least six times after we have already tucked her in. I feel that we spend our evenings running in and out of her room. She has a lot of different reasons for calling us: she needs a drink of water, the closet door is open, she needs a night light, she can't stop all of the scary thoughts in her head. This goes on anywhere from thirty minutes to two hours. Just when I think she is finally asleep, she calls again.

Falling Asleep

It sounds like your daughter has you and your wife well trained to jump at the sound of her voice. The three of you need to work together to make a bedtime plan. Some weekend afternoon sit down together and make a written list of every reason your daughter uses to get you back into her room. Have her circle all of the things she could take care of herself. At eight years old she can certainly get a drink of water, shut her closet door, turn on a night light, and perform any other similar task. Let her know that all of these things are her responsibilities and that you are not going to do them again.

It is important for your daughter to know that adults, too, sometimes have trouble falling asleep. The quiet darkness can set the stage for one's mind to race with thoughts, and some of them can be scary. Talk with her about ways to make the scary thoughts go away. One way is simply to order the thoughts to go away; not all children can do this successfully, but many can once the idea has been suggested to them. Another way is to concentrate on something else. Suggest, for example, that she paint a mental picture of something special and then change all of the colors in the picture. Or ask her about the most beautiful place she has ever seen and assure her that she can travel there in her own head whenever she chooses. Or tell her to tighten and then relax the muscles all over her body.

It is important to help your daughter learn about various ways to prepare for sleep. It will take all of you working together to create a better ending to the day.

Getting up in the Night

I hope you can settle an argument that is causing friction between my husband and me. Our seven-year-old son was close to my husband's mother, who died last month. Ever since, our son gets up in the night crying and wants to sleep in our bed. Until now, our son had always been a good sleeper, and my husband says we are going to set him back if we give in to him now. I can't stand fighting about this in the middle of the night, and I don't know what is right.

A very real reason has prompted this present disruption. Even though your son's behavior will probably return to normal in a short time, this is a very difficult period for him, and he will need help from both you and your husband.

You should give your son a chance during the day to express his feelings about his grandmother. Encourage him to think about her, and to talk about her. If this causes him to cry, tell him it is natural to show pain over the loss of a loved one, and that he should let the tears come because they will help the pain go away.

When children experience the death of someone close to them, they often become fearful about the other family members dying, so you might want to discuss this with your son also.

There are a number of books available on the death of a grandparent. You might want to get one of these from the public library and read it together. (Look in the card catalog under the subject-heading of "Death.")

If your son keeps his feelings inside during the day he may continue to try to release them at night. When he comes into your room at night, go back with him to his room and stay with him until he falls back asleep. Or you might have a sleeping bag on your floor for him.

It is extremely difficult to get my six-year-old daughter up in time for school in the morning. I go into her room, open the windows, tell her "good morning," and pull down the covers. She groans, shoves me away, and goes back to sleep. Every school day starts this way!

Waking up in the Morning

It is hard to have sleep end abruptly, and it's cozy under those blankets. Your present wake-up plan clearly is not working, so you will want to find an entirely different approach. At dinner one evening, have a wrapped package at your daughter's place. The card might read, "For a very special girl who is ready to be her very own boss." Inside the package she will find her own alarm clock. If possible, get her a clock-radio, so she can wake up to the calm sound of music; this will be a gentle way to disrupt her sleep. Tell her that you know she will get up when the alarm goes off. Help her to feel proud of herself for taking over this important responsibility.

Suggestions made in this section are intended to encourage the assessment of daily routines that might need changing, using simple solutions whenever possible. Recognizing real causes for sleep disruptions and working on them is important. Whenever parents realize they are being manipulated, they need to set firm but loving limits. If possible, children should be given the opportunity to work with their parents for constructive resolutions.

EATING

In theory, mealtime should be a pleasant time for family members; in practice, the dinner table often becomes a battleground. Power struggles concerning food can lead to habitual bickering between parents and children, and indigestion for the entire family. As children grow and change, so do the potential mealtime problems. The following concerns are typical.

Feeding a Young Child

I don't see how my three-year-old daughter can survive on as little as she eats, though she seems healthy and happy enough. When I try to put something in her mouth at the dinner table, she spits it out. I try to coax her to eat more, but she ignores me.

As soon as babies have the finger dexterity to feed themselves, adults should stop feeding them. A logical way to help children feel independent and self-sufficient is to allow them to be in charge of their own mouths. Some children do not require large amounts of food in order to grow normally or stay healthy. Do not try to put food into your daughter's mouth or to coax her to eat more. At three years old she is perfectly capable of feeding herself, and you should try to avoid creating food-related problems.

Problems Caused by Dessert

Our four-and-a-half-year-old son begins asking "What's for dessert?" before we even sit down for dinner. My husband insists that our son eat everything on his plate or he can't have dessert. Last night my husband ended up spanking our son and sending him to his room because he kept whining and nagging about dessert. Our dinner hour has become totally disrupted by a continuing battle of wills between my husband and son. What can I do? How can I make dinnertime more pleasant for my family and myself?

In a calm, happy moment, discuss this situation with your husband and ask him to join you in searching for constructive solutions. Here are several suggestions:

Let all members of your family put food on their own plates. This way they select exactly the amount they feel they can eat.

One evening, put the desserts in paper bags and place a bag under each seat before dinner. Have a previous pact with your husband that he will not take this away from your son no matter how little he eats. Have a previous pact with your son to refrain from mentioning dessert during the meal. The fact that your son knows the dessert is securely under his seat should help him to be less concerned.

Another evening, serve dessert at the beginning of the meal and call it a "backward dinner."

Alleviating your son's dessert anxiety and your husband's punitive role should make mealtime a lot more pleasant. It is important to stop using desserts as rewards. Sweets can become far too important, and your goal is to establish healthy eating habits.

Food Preferences

My seven-year-old has narrowed down the foods she will eat to four choices: peanut butter, bananas, scrambled eggs, and grapes. Do you think she should be eating a much larger variety?

It is understandable that you feel frustrated over your daughter's limited food choices, but since she has selected nutritious foods you shouldn't be too disturbed. A lot of children go through periods of strong food preferences. These periods usually pass swiftly if parents don't make an issue out of the child's behavior. Your daughter has chosen foods that are soft and easy to chew and swallow. At seven she might have a number of loose teeth and these foods make eating easier. Do not take her rejection of something you have fixed as a personal affront. As she observes everyone else enjoying other foods, she will eventually return to a diet with more variety.

After-school Snacks

Lately my son has been fixing elaborate after-school snacks. When it's time for dinner he isn't hungry. I am glad that he is interested in cooking, but what can I do about our family dinners?

Perhaps your family dinners could be scheduled for a

later time. Another solution would be smaller after-school snacks for your son. To encourage his interest in cooking, ask him to create dishes for dinner. The whole family would be able to enjoy sampling his food.

Bored at Dinner

We have three children and trying to have a family dinner has turned into a real problem. My husband and I resent the fact that our nine-year-old daughter continually looks at her watch and acts bored. From time to time she pokes her younger brother or sister to begin a fight. How can we have pleasant family meals?

Many families report boredom setting in around the dinner table. You might want to think of some creative ways to spark up a few meals a week. You could have a dress-up, candlelit dinner or plan to eat on a picnic tablecloth placed on the floor of a room where you have never served a meal. One morning, ask each member of your family to think up a question for everyone to answer at dinner. This could enliven the mealtime conversation, as it would be interesting to hear their questions and the answers.

Preparing School Lunches

Several times each week, our daughter complains about the school lunches my husband and I take turns making for her. She is only eight, but we are thinking about telling her to make her own lunches. Do you think she is old enough to handle this?

You and your husband have a good idea. Let your daughter make her own lunches, not as a punishment but because you feel sure she can handle this responsibility. When this routine is a regular part of your daughter's schedule, offer to make lunch for her once in a while. Chances are, she'll really appreciate your efforts rather than complain. Be sure to praise her along the way for doing such a fine job.

My son is obese, a problem I had always hoped to avoid. I have three other children who look just fine, and I keep food around the house that they like. The problem is that my son will go on binges, eating everything he can find. I am really upset over this, and I don't know where to turn.

Overweight

You haven't mentioned visiting your regular doctor to find out if your son really should be classified as "obese." Because you have always dreaded having an obese child you might be mistaking a case of being slightly overweight with one of obesity. In any event, this is difficult for you, and you want to do something about it.

Obesity is a serious problem for children and those who care about them. Obese children quickly learn that adults generally are sorry for them but that peers exclude them. Obesity can hamper a child's ability to participate successfully in many activities. The most important issue is that obesity is detrimental to the child's health and self-image.

Ask your other children to help. Tell them that you are going to buy only nutritious food for snacks, and that you trust they will not complain but understand it's really better for their bodies, too. Prepare very good but low-calorie meals. Do not nag or show disgust toward your son. Rather, let him know how much you care about him no matter what he weighs. Try to find a pattern in his eating binges; they might occur, for example, when he feels bored or upset about his school experiences. If you can get him involved in an activity, the problem might solve itself. This activity could be a hobby (making models, taking care of a pet, collecting stamps—it doesn't matter what, as long as it interests him) or a neighborhood job (cutting grass, washing cars, etc.). And, above all, find the time to give him attention on matters unrelated to his problem.

I am raising my twelve-year-old daughter on my own. The other night I saw a TV program on eating disorders, and

Underweight

*one of the persons on the program talked about kids want-
ing to lose weight so much that they actually kill themselves. It got me to thinking about my daughter. She wears
loose clothes so it's hard to tell, but I think she is too thin.
Maybe she has this problem, but I don't have a wife to
check this out with.*

Worrying about being thin has led to anorexia nervosa
and other eating disorders, particularly in girls. The
simplest solution would be to ask your doctor to see
her and then discuss it with both of you. Perhaps there
isn't a real problem. But if there is, you don't want to
ignore it. In many communities there are organizations
that sponsor meetings for single parents. At the meetings, members exchange ideas on the raising of children and relate experiences they have had. You might
find such a group beneficial, as it would enable you
to discuss problems with parents whose situation is
similar to your own.

This section encouraged parents to look for swift and creative solutions to
eating problems. Eating is an area where children can and do show their
independence, and parents need to respect this. Mealtime is often the only
time the whole family is together. It is worth the time and energy to try
to make this a pleasant experience for everyone.

CLOTHING

Shopping for clothes and selecting which clothes to wear each day can be
a continual source of friction between parents and their children. There are
many factors involved in picking out clothes to buy. A child's level of
physical development affects his or her ability to get dressed and undressed.
It is important not to frustrate your child with apparel that is too difficult
to handle; on the other hand, don't underestimate the child's potential.
Whenever possible, it is a good idea to let children try putting things on
and taking them off before you make the purchase.

Parents and children often have two different ideas about the selection
of clothing. Children might focus on how the outfit looks and how it feels
against their skin. They may pick out clothes that they have seen their
friends wearing. Generally, the parents have a different set of concerns.
These include durability, safety, appearance, fit, and ease of care. Every-

one's concerns should be respected, but this does not always make shopping an easy task.

My son has attached himself to one shirt and one pair of pants. He insists on wearing them every day, even if they are dirty. I never imagined a four-year-old could be so stubborn. He throws a major tantrum if I refuse to let him wear them. He has many other nice clothes he could wear instead.

Preference for One Outfit

You picked a perfect word to describe a stage many young children go through; your son is "attached" to one particular outfit, and he might outgrow the outfit before he outgrows his attachment to it. If you realize that he has a specific preference, it is a good idea to buy a duplicate outfit. Sometimes this isn't possible, and parents find themselves washing out the favorite set of clothes every night. If you can handle it, this is a good time to respect your child's choice and honor it. There will be many other, more serious issues to fight over.

My five-year-old son appears every morning fully clothed for the day. While I am happy that he likes to dress himself, I am unhappy over his choices. He combines colors that do not go together, and I find myself frowning when I see him rather than welcoming the day with a smile.

Coordinating Colors

No one will judge your skills as a parent by what your son wears. However, it is obviously very important to you to have your son wear color-coordinated outfits. Rather than being unhappy every time you look at him, find ways to solve the problem so you'll both be happy. One suggestion is color coding hangers in your son's closet. Wrap colored tape around the top of the hanger to show which colors go together. For example: pants hung on a hanger with yellow tape should be worn only with shirts on hangers also marked with yellow tape. Another approach would be to stack co-ordinated outfits together on a shelf. Your son could pick any outfit he felt like wearing as long as all the clothes came from the same stack.

Changing Clothes All Day

My daughter is six and I feel like I am running her personal laundry. She changes clothes from morning to night. Some of the things she takes off end up in the laundry hamper. Others she leaves in a variety of places, including the floor. I have told her over and over again to stop this, but she doesn't.

Many children go through a phase of constantly changing clothes. It is understandable why you are upset. When we tell children the same thing over and over again without getting the results we want, it is a signal to find a new approach. Tell your daughter that you have been thinking about how capable she is and that you have two new family jobs you want her to take on: the first is helping you with the actual laundry process, the second is serving as an official inspector. Give her a badge with the word "Inspector" written on it, and have her check all of her clothes to see which ones are really dirty and which ones could be folded, put away, and worn again. Have her make a pile of everything that is clean and then help her put it away. The idea is to create a team effort, not to impose a punishment. When you have less laundry as a result of this plan, take the extra time to do something special with your daughter. As you play a game or read a book—whatever the two of you have chosen—be sure to tell her *why* you have the time. You'll both feel good about solving this problem.

Peer Pressure

I cannot remember my clothes preferences as a ten-year-old, but I do know my daughter's: she insists on wearing the exact kind of clothes her friends wear. She even wants to shop at the same stores they go to. She doesn't look good in some of the styles her friends wear, but that doesn't bother her as long as they match what her friends are wearing.

Many children, as they become more social, want to wear clothes just like their friends wear. Our adult brains tell us "This is ridiculous," but, as you indicate, we have forgotten this phase in our own lives. Hating what a parent makes you wear, looking different from one's peers, imagining that everyone is laughing at you—all of these cause emotional pain. Whenever possible, it is wise to value the child's choice, as this phase will pass.

This section offered a number of guidelines for selecting children's clothes. Most important in this respect is the child's preferences. Personal preference and, later, peer approval often will dictate the kinds of clothes children want to wear. Respecting their choices can help develop their decision-making ability and avoid having costly, unworn clothes in the closet.

THE BATHROOM

For children to really like themselves, it is important for them to like their bodies. Without realizing it, we easily give children negative messages about their bodies. We have all heard parents say, "Keep your fingers out of your mouth!" or "How disgusting! You know you're not supposed to pick your nose!" These things feel good and would be fine if the child did them privately. The parent's task is to teach the appropriate and inappropriate places for exploring one's body. Negative messages seem all too easy to convey, so it is important to find ways to convey positive feelings about bodies. Just as we often praise our children when they are wearing something brand new, we need to praise them when they are wearing nothing at all. We might simply say, "Be sure to take a look at yourself in the mirror. Your body is beautiful!"

The most natural time to help children appreciate their physical selves is during daily routines in the bathroom. We can help even our very young children to accept their bodies. We communicate these positive messages through what we say and how we say it and by finding appropriate ways to help children take care of themselves.

My son is two, and he seems totally uninterested in using the toilet. I ask him a hundred times a day if he needs to   **Using the Toilet** *use it, but he always says no. Several of his friends are already finished with diapers, so I know he is old enough.*

There is a wide range of ages when children begin using the toilet. Many children are well over three before they are completely toilet trained. Try to avoid comparing your son to other children, because each child is unique. Undoubtedly, your son can do some other things that his friends have not mastered.

You should not have to ask your son continually if he needs to go to the bathroom. Instead, you should concentrate on helping him recognize the signals his body will give him. He will probably be encouraged to use the toilet when he sees his friends using it. You can certainly suggest to him that he will soon be in control of his body and will be able to throw the diapers away.

It is important to avoid a power stuggle over toilet training. Try to relax, and feel assured that it will happen soon and it will happen naturally.

Withholding Bowel Movements

My four-year-old daughter refuses to have bowel movements, often withholding them for as long as a week. The doctor said this is not good for her body. I sit in the bathroom and read to her for almost an hour sometimes, but she still doesn't move her bowels. Once in a while she cries because her stomach hurts. Her father and I keep bringing up the problem, but she doesn't want to discuss it. This didn't happen with any of her brothers or sisters, so we really don't know what to do.

Perhaps your daughter has found that by withholding her bowel movements she gets a lot of special attention. Since she has made it clear that she doesn't want to talk about this problem, why don't you tell her a little story when you are having a cozy chat (not in the bathroom). The story might sound like this: "Once upon a time, there was a little girl who lived in a big family. Everyone was busy, so there wasn't much quiet time. The best time in the whole day was when

Mommy or Daddy read to the little girl while she sat on the toilet. One day, Mommy and Daddy decided it was silly to read to their daughter in the bathroom. They thought it would be much more comfortable to read in a rocking chair or in bed. So from that day on, they read outside of the bathroom and they all liked it better."

You mentioned that you have been in touch with your doctor. Next time you take your daughter in for a checkup, drop a note to the doctor ahead of time, asking him or her to tell your daughter that her body is just perfect and that she isn't going to have a problem with her bowels for very long.

If a child is in good physical condition, eats a proper diet, gets enough exercise and sleep, and feels loved, then the problem of withholding bowel movements can be solved. Read to your daughter outside of the bathroom, and stop talking about her problem. Let her take charge of what does or doesn't happen on the toilet, and intervene only if she comes to you for help.

Bedwetting

Until recently, when he entered the first grade, my six-year-old son never had a problem getting to the toilet in time. Now he has suddenly started wetting the bed at night. He could hardly wait to be in first grade, and everything else is going really well. We have cut out juice and milk during the evening, but we don't know what else to do.

Some children begin bed-wetting when they experience stress. Adjusting to first grade could be the cause in your son's case, or he might be so tired from the new schedule that he's having a more difficult time feeling the bladder pressure during a sound sleep.

You don't sound alarmed, and that's good. That wouldn't help your son to conquer the problem. Remind him that he has already shown that he can control his body through the night and assure him that the bed-wetting is only temporary. If the bed-wetting goes on for several months, then you should not remain so casual about it. Your son might then need more help. Ask him if he wants you to wake him to use the toilet before you go to sleep. The most important thing is for your son to feel that he is in control of his body.

Cleanliness

My daughter used to enjoy all of the bathroom chores, but now she tries to avoid them. She doesn't want to bother washing her hands, and she feels brushing her teeth is a waste of time. When I insist on putting her in the bathtub for a good scrubbing, she objects. My patience is running out.

It sounds as if your daughter is successfully frustrating you. Taking care of one's body should be a joy, not a "chore" or a source of conflict. Perhaps you need a few new approaches. Your daughter is old enough to understand the reasons for personal hygiene. You might want to create a game or a quiz about what happens to people who ignore their bodies. Talk about what can happen when hygiene is poor. For example, unwashed hands could place germs or pinworms in your mouth. Unbrushed teeth lead to bad breath and eventual cavities. You might take a stack of index cards and put the name of a body part on one card and the consequences of neglect on another. Then ask your daughter to see how fast she can match them. Do not give her a lecture about any of these cards—she'll get the message on her own.

You might also try letting your daughter pick a new kind of soap, shampoo, or toothpaste. She might enjoy using these self-selected items. Refrain from "putting her in the bathtub for a good scrubbing." At seven, she is perfectly capable of cleaning herself. You should not handle her in an angry or punitive way. If she wants to play baby and have you take care of her for one bathing, then gently wash her.

Finally, it is important to communicate to your daughter that you like taking care of your own body. Children learn a lot through observation and imitation.

When my son was little, I brushed his teeth for him. Some- **Brushing Teeth**
how we haven't broken this habit, and now my wife feels
he's far too old to be helped and should do it himself.

It's nice that you have been a part of this dental care
routine for so long, but children must be taught to take
care of themselves as they grow older. Perhaps you
could begin to break the habit by playing and having
some fun. For example, both of you could brush your
teeth at the same time. Or you might copy the exact
way your son brushes his teeth and then have him
copy you. Another variation would be to each try
brushing your teeth with your nondominant hand.

Do ten-year-olds need a lot of time alone in the bathroom? **Privacy**
My daughter used to take a reasonable amount of time
there, and she didn't care if I came in to get things. Now
she wants the door locked, and she seems to take forever.

Children begin requesting privacy in the bathroom at
different ages. Respecting this need is a perfect way
to let children know that their bodies belong to them.
At ten, your daughter might be very preoccupied with
the changes beginning to take place in her body. She
also probably has more interest in how she looks and
spends a lot of time fussing with her hair. Be sure to
compliment her efforts when she comes out.
    Perhaps you can help your daughter to pick more
convenient times to lock herself in the bathroom. If
you or another family member does need something,
ask her to hand it out. You might need to help her
identify a reasonable amount of time to occupy the
bathroom. By allowing her to participate in setting the
rules, you will demonstrate your respect for this young
lady.

Included in this section were thoughts on giving children positive messages
about their bodies, avoiding power struggles about bodily care, and encouraging children to participate in making decisions about their own bodies. It is important to let children do as much as possible for themselves

and to respect their requests for privacy. All of these issues are foundations for developing self-esteem.

MEDICAL ISSUES

Good health, illness, doctors, and dentists—the whole area of medical care is important in helping children take care of their bodies. The self-protection section of this chapter emphasizes teaching children that their bodies belong to them. How can we help children to understand and accept the necessary invasion of their bodies when we take them to the doctor or the dentist?

You can help prepare children for visits to the doctor in many ways. Long before your child can understand your words, he or she will understand your tone of voice. Explain, even to your infant, why you are going to the doctor. When you call to make a routine medical appointment, ask the receptionist to check your child's chart and tell you what medical procedures will be performed. Then, prepare your child for the visit. For example, if you learned that your child will need an inoculation, give him or her a brief explanation on the way to the doctor's office. Tell your child that the disease the injection prevents is far more serious than the temporary pain the injection causes. Be sure to ask whether your child has any questions. One little boy heard the doctor say she was going to inject dye into his vein. Terrified, he whispered to his mother, "Why does the doctor want me to die?" Misconceptions can be corrected if you find out what your child is thinking.

If you learn that the doctor is going to ask for a urine sample, try to get the sample at home and take it to the office with you. It is less frightening for a child to collect urine at home than in the doctor's office. Putting urine in a cup is confusing to a child who has been told that urine belongs in the toilet. Be sure to explain that urine in test tubes and under microscopes can tell the doctor a lot about how a body is doing inside.

The following pages contain a number of concerns and suggestions about doctors, dentists, hospitals, illnesses, and surgery.

Selecting a Doctor   *My son's pediatrician has an excellent reputation as a doctor, but his personality leaves a lot to be desired. When my son realizes we are heading for this doctor's office, he gets nervous and usually cries. I have noticed that even the receptionist and nurse appear afraid of the doctor, and I have heard him yelling at them. He is not at all patient with my son's emotional reaction to him. Should I stick* *with this doctor because I know he is outstanding from a medical standpoint, or should I try to find another one? The truth is, I don't know how to find someone better.*

You probably do need to find someone else. First, however, you might drop your present pediatrician a note or make an appointment to talk with him. Tell him that you appreciate his medical expertise but are concerned about your son's reactions to office visits. This type of contact can sometimes dramatically change a doctor's relationship with a child. He might make a real effort to make your son feel at ease during subsequent visits. If there isn't a substantial change, then you should look for someone else.

It is worth considerable time and energy to look for a doctor who seems right for you and your child. There are a number of questions to consider:

- ☐ Did someone you respect refer you to this doctor?
- ☐ How comfortable do you feel with the office personnel?
- ☐ What is the physical environment of the office like? Is it appealing to children?
- ☐ Is it difficult or easy to get an appointment? Ask other parents about this and about how long they usually spend in the waiting room.
- ☐ Do children with contagious illnesses wait in the waiting room, or are they admitted to examining rooms right away? Ask the receptionist.
- ☐ Who is on call when the doctor is unavailable, and how often does this occur?
- ☐ Does the doctor make emergency home visits?
- ☐ Does he or she seem willing to listen to you?
- ☐ Does the doctor ask you pertinent questions?
- ☐ What is the doctor's hospital affiliation? Is the hospital conveniently located? What is its reputation as a hospital for children?
- ☐ How does the doctor feel about children and parents actively participating in health care? Does he or she explain why things should be done, or simply issue orders? How does he or she feel about parents' staying in hospital rooms with their children?

These are some of the important guidelines in selecting a doctor for your child. However, it takes a few visits to know if the doctor's performance meets your expectations. You should observe your child's interactions with the doctor. It is important for parents and children to look forward to seeing their doctors.

Doctors as a Child Matures

My daughter has always loved our pediatrician, but recently she has begged me not to make an appointment for a routine checkup. She is eleven and beginning to develop, and she has firmly stated that she will not get undressed in his office. When I remind her about how much she likes him and jokes with him, she claims she is "too old" to see a pediatrician unless she is ill. I believe in routine checkups as an important part of health care, but I also want to respect my daughter's strong feelings. Obviously, I feel torn.

You are correct in respecting your daughter's feelings. Early adolescence is a time for many physical changes, and they are often accompanied by requests for increased privacy. For now, perhaps, the doctor will agree to let your daughter remain dressed during checkups. Another possibility is to find a woman doctor for your daughter.

Selecting a Dentist

As a child I always dreaded visits to the dentist, and I still feel that way as an adult. Is there anything I can do to prevent my children from feeling this way?

Many of the suggestions about how to select a pediatrician also apply when selecting a dentist. A helpful approach is to make several "get-acquainted" visits with your child before dental work actually begins; even if the dentist charges for these visits (some do, others don't), it will be well worth it. You might suggest taking a favorite doll or stuffed animal along for a dental checkup. Using these special friends, the dentist can help a child understand what needs to be done and why. Many children like to go along and watch their parents or older brothers or sisters in the dentist's chair and then request a turn for themselves. By all means, select a dentist who cares about your child's feelings.

Taking my son to the dentist is a real ordeal. He starts crying the minute we get to the building and has a full-blown temper tantrum in the waiting room. By the time he gets into the dentist's chair, I am exhausted, embarrassed, and furious.

Temper Tantrums in the Dentist's Office

Your reactions to this draining experience seem natural. Before your next visit, there are a few steps you might take. Call your local dental association or dental school and request free brochures on dental care for children. Also ask for pictures of teeth that haven't had proper dental care. Your goal in showing your son these pictures would not be to scare him into accepting the need for regular, preventive dental care: emphasize that none of you will have the problems depicted because you take such good care of your teeth. Accept your son's fear of the dentist. Don't chide him for his tears, but try to help him control them.

Talk with the receptionist about your problem, and request the first morning appointment so your son can be taken in the minute you get to the office. The waiting room time probably makes him more anxious, which leads to his emotional outbursts. As you walk into the building, tell your son that you think he is going to handle the situation a lot better this time. Describe the new behavior that you think you will see and how happy you both will be about this change. This will let him know that there is an alternative to the temper tantrum routine.

I really hate to call my child's doctor on weekends or during the night. However, sometimes my child is too sick to wait, and then I find myself a nervous wreck on the telephone.

Calling the Doctor

After the conversation has ended, I think of other things I should have said, but I don't think well under pressure.

If you feel your child is ill enough to warrant calling the doctor, then dismiss your guilt feelings. An important part of being a doctor is being available outside of office hours. Children cannot schedule illness for the convenience of a doctor. Before you place the call, there are some steps you could take to lessen your nervousness on the telephone. Write down a list of all the symptoms you have noted, and be sure to check your child's temperature. Have the phone number of your pharmacy ready, along with paper and pen to write down any instructions the doctor might give you. At the beginning of the conversation, be sure to state your child's age, as it is impossible for a doctor to remember the age of every patient. Your major focus must be a swift recovery for your child. If the doctor's help is indicated, by all means request it!

Caring for a Sick Child

When any of my children are sick it seems to bring out the worst in me. I'm stuck in the apartment, and I get up many times during the night because they call for me or because I want to check on them. During the day I feel overtired and like a prisoner in my own apartment.

Illness does cause dramatic changes in routines. If you have a friend or relative who could come in for a few hours, it would be good for you to take a break. Try also to think of some things to do with your child that might be interesting for you. It is a good idea to have a "secret shelf" with a few books, games, art supplies, and records that are pulled out only during these times. Your children may spend long periods of time entertaining themselves with these rarely used items. When you join in, the activities will be fun for you as well.

Find ways to involve your child in his or her own care. Make a chart showing what time medicine needs to be taken. Set an alarm for these times, and let your child notify you when it goes off. Write a story together about the world's greatest patient. Begin with the physical and verbal warning signals that an illness was coming. Draw pictures of the germs that have invaded the healthy cells. Then write down everything being done to get rid of the infection. Your child is the star of this story, the center of the medical team involved in this drama of illness and recovery. You might each want to make daily predictions about when partial and then total recovery will occur. Your homemade book can note the anger you and your child have felt about the illness, but the overall tone should be positive, reminding the young patient that most of the time his or her body is perfectly healthy.

Hanging on to Illness

My daughter seems to enjoy being sick because I give her so much attention and her father stops on his way home from work to buy her little get-well gifts. When I feel she is well enough to return to school, she always begs to stay home for at least one more day.

While you want to make your child as happy as possible when she is sick, you must be careful not to make illness more attractive than health. Your daughter is smart enough to want to hold on to the attention and privileges of illness. Tell her about something special you want to do with her when she returns from her first day back at school. Be sure to spend at least a small amount of time alone with her each day when she is well. You might suggest that your husband bring her a "so glad you are so healthy" gift once in a while.

Accidents

Whenever my little one falls down, I feel like I have to run to her to make sure she is okay. Most of the time she's fine, but I'm afraid that the one time I don't get to her she'll really be injured. My mother says I am overly cautious and it isn't good for my daughter.

We do not have to raise our children as we were raised, but sometimes the objectivity a grandparent offers can be helpful. The next time you are near a group of very young children, watch what happens when they fall. They usually look to their parents for a reaction. If a parent seems anxious or upset or comes running, the child starts crying whether or not he or she is hurt. If the parent smiles and in a cheerful voice says, "You fell down," the child probably laughs, gets up, and returns to playing.

Your daughter will take her lead on how to behave from you. You should not encourage her to cry or worry about every fall. You will recognize cries of real pain, which are quite different from the run-of-the-mill "I feel sorry for myself" cries. In the event of a real accident and injury, it is important for you to stay calm. If both you and the child are hysterical, you cannot find out what is wrong and get the necessary help. Be sure to keep emergency numbers and addresses near your telephone. But, though you must be prepared, remember that most children grow up without having serious accidents.

Preparation for Surgery

Our four-year-old daughter has been having trouble with her tonsils and adenoids for several years, but knowing how terrified she would be of surgery, her pediatrician and I have put off an operation as long as possible. Her condition is getting worse, however, and he has scheduled her for surgery in two weeks. How can I prepare her without making her more scared than she already is?

You and the doctor were wise to have waited as long as possible. Your daughter is now old enough to share her feelings and to discuss the surgery with you. At four she can recognize the effects of illness. Knowledge is the most important foundation for her hospitalization. Here are some of the many possible ways to prepare a child for surgery:

☐ Visit the hospital to meet the staff and to see the physical environment.
☐ Read library books and pamphlets about the kind of surgery your child will undergo.
☐ Ask the doctor questions that you and your child have prepared ahead of time.

☐ Spend some time with a child who has had the same kind of surgery. Your child might have some questions to ask, but the important thing will be for her to see that the other child is fine. Decide together which special treasures to take to the hospital—perhaps a stuffed animal, a toy, or a photograph.

☐ Use dramatic play to act out the surgery with dolls.

You will not want to spend the entire two weeks dwelling on this issue; that would make everyone more anxious. Use your own good judgment about when to bring the subject up, but always respond when your daughter raises it. Details about injections, being put to sleep, and possible pain will help to prepare your child. This information removes some of the shock of the reality and also builds trust between parent and child. Probably the best time to provide this information would be a few days before the surgery.

Remember that this surgery is not a choice, it is a necessity. Be very clear in your own mind that all of you are working together to help your daughter have a healthy body. As you prepare her with a positive attitude, you might decrease your own weepy feelings by removing both of your fears.

Staying with Hospitalized Child

My six-year-old son is going to be hospitalized for about four days after surgery. I want to stay with him the whole time, and my boss has agreed to give me the time off work. The doctor feels it isn't necessary for me to be there, but he will tell the hospital staff to let me stay if I insist. He said that many parents interfere with the nurses' routines and that children tend to cry more if their parents are around. I feel I belong with my son, but I don't want to make it harder for him.

Follow your instincts. The reassurance of having a parent in the room can make hospitalization less frightening, while separation during this time can aggravate emotional turmoil. The only exception would be for parents who are hysterical and unable to control their emotions. Many hospitals still refuse to let parents stay with their children. Fortunately, you have a doctor who will back up your wishes and a hospital staff who will agree. Be prepared for the staff to ignore you initially, but don't take it personally. Remember that you are there for your child. Even if all you do is stand and watch others care for your son, he knows that you are sharing the experience with him. Many parents have reported "proving themselves" to the staff and eventually feeling included in the team effort to help the child. The doctor is right that your son might cry more, but that's because he feels safe enough to reveal his inner feelings. It is better to release the tears than to hold them inside.

Delayed Reaction to Surgery

When our daughter needed surgery, my husband and I answered all of her questions honestly. She is very bright and has a vocabulary far beyond her eight years. She amazed everyone in the hospital with her understanding of the surgery and her perfect behavior. We did notice some babyish behavior when she came home, but it seemed to pass. Now, three months later, she has started having nightmares about strange people coming into our home and hurting her. Could this be related to the surgery after so many months? We don't know what to do.

Many children demonstrate delayed reactions to traumatic experiences. Your daughter's dreams about strange people invading and hurting her is probably an unconscious interpretation of what happened in the hospital. In her dreams, she is working out the anxiety she must have felt and ignored while being a model citizen in the hospital. She acted mature beyond her years, and now, three months later, she feels safe enough to begin reacting to the experience.

Ask your daughter questions about her time in the hospital. Tell her that it is natural that she found the experience scary. If she doesn't want to talk about it, perhaps you can find another means of expression for her to use—hand puppets or paints, for example. A frightening experience can become increasingly upsetting if only the negative aspects are recalled, so be sure to remind her of the positive side—of how she cooperated with the medical team and healed swiftly because she took good care of herself. Any pleasant or funny incidents are worth recalling. These opportunities to release inner tensions should eliminate the nightmares.

This section has emphasized the careful selection of doctors and dentists and the importance of giving children honest explanations about illness and medical procedures. It is essential that children share the responsibility for keeping their bodies healthy.

SEXUALITY

Children learn about sex from their parents' actions and attitudes, not just their words. The tone of the message is far more important than its wording or the approach used. A positive attitude on the part of the parents is vital to a child's appreciation of his or her own body. This section points out some opportunities for expressing acceptance.

Sex Play

Last weekend my daughter had a girlfriend over for the night, and I heard them giggling quite late. I went in to tell them it was time to sleep, and these two seven-year-olds were undressed and looking at each other with flashlights. I just told them to go to sleep, and they put on their pajamas and settled down. I really wasn't sure what else to say.

It is good that you didn't get angry or punitive about the sex play you saw. You were matter-of-fact about the late hour and the need to go to sleep. Children often play "doctor" or find some other way to learn about their own and other's bodies. While you wouldn't want your daughter to spend all of her time at sex play, it is natural for young children to participate in these explorations. The next time you stumble into a similar game, you could say "Bodies are really interesting to see but right now it is time for sleeping."

Interrupting Parents' Lovemaking

The other night when my husband and I went to bed we thought the children were asleep. We were in the midst of lovemaking when our five-year-old son threw open our door and walked in. We were so shocked that we didn't know what to say.

After that experience, you'll probably want to put a lock on your door to protect your lovemaking privacy. At some future date your son will probably try to enter your room only to discover the door is locked. Simply tell him that you two are having a "private time."

Nudity

We have three children, a two-year-old son and daughters aged four and seven. My husband has always taken showers with the children, but lately our seven-year-old says she wants to take them alone. My husband wants to continue family showers and when I ask him to respect our daughter's wishes he says I am "interfering" in his relationship with the children.

Even if your husband feels you are interfering, you need to explain that your daughter should feel that she can make decisions about her own body. The importance of this feeling is described in the self-protection section of this chapter. When your husband understands it, he will undoubtedly want your daughter to have her way. Each couple has to make its own decisions about nudity in front of children. At times, children are bound to walk in when their parents are dressing or undressing. This is quite different from intentional nudity. Many child-development experts believe it is preferable for children to learn about physical differences by observing siblings and peers. Adult bodies are fully developed and could lead children to wonder why their own genitals are so different. Also, children have strong feelings about their parents and become confused when these feelings are complicated by sexual excitement.

The other night I was fixing dinner when I heard my mother-in-law say "Stop it." When I walked in to find out what was going on, she had a look of disgust on her face and her hands were over her eyes. My three-year-old daughter was straddled on the arm of the couch rubbing herself back and forth. My mother-in-law believes that masturbation can lead to mental illness. She also said I should start questioning my eleven-year-old son, who is spending increasing amounts of time in the bathroom. This wasn't a very pleasant experience for any of us, and we want to avoid it in the future. My husband wants to tell his mother to keep her mouth shut, but I'm not sure he should.

Masturbation

Chances are that even if your mother-in-law refrains from saying something in the future she will still communicate nonverbally. Years ago some people did believe that masturbation could lead to mental disorders. This is not true. As a matter of fact, the only potentially serious consequence is the feeling of shame or guilt that may arise.

Masturbation usually begins somewhere during the second year of life. At this point, many children discover the pleasurable feeling of rubbing against something rhythmically. This practice is normal and harmless, and children should not be threatened, scolded, or made to feel frightened about it.

Your daughter certainly saw and heard her grandmother's reactions. In a very simple way, explain that Grandma doesn't like children to touch themselves, but that you and Daddy think it's okay. Touching is a way to find out more about parts of the body. Explain, though, that some other people feel the way Grandma does, so it is better for your daughter not to touch herself in the presence of others.

Grandma's insinuation about your son may or may not be accurate. He is eleven, and many boys this age spend more time grooming themselves than in the past. If indeed he is masturbating in the bathroom, then he has already discovered an appropriate private place for this activity. There is no reason for you to investigate or interfere.

Negative Attitude about Sex

I have a terrific nine-year-old daughter. I have always answered her questions about sex with love and honesty. The other day I noticed that she was scowling at me and she clearly had something on her mind, so I asked her about it. She blurted out, "You and Daddy do 'it'! Sex is sick and disgusting." I was so shocked at the content of this outburst that I was absolutely speechless. What could I have said?

You and your daughter seem to have a good foundation for discussing any issue that might upset her. Because of your honest and loving answers to her questions, your daughter trusts you enough to express a very negative thought. It is also obvious that you are attentive to her nonverbal messages. Children often find it difficult to communicate messages that they consider very upsetting.

By all means accept your daughter's feelings and try to understand why she has them. She might be feeling frightened and vulnerable because her body is on the verge of going through some major changes. Growing up is something many children both fear and happily anticipate. You could specifically respond to her outburst by saying, "I know it sounds sick to you— I felt the same way when I was your age. But when you really love someone, lovemaking is wonderful. I am thankful that Daddy and I loved each other enough to get married and eventually have you. If we had never made love together, you wouldn't be here, and you are very special to us."

Nocturnal Emissions ("Wet Dreams")

For the past few weeks our eleven-year-old son has been up one or two times a week in the middle of the night. He puts his sheet in the washing machine and then the dryer, and then he takes a shower. I assume that he's having wet dreams and is ashamed. But I told him about wet dreams over a year ago and assured him they were perfectly natural. What should I do next?

Even though you talked about it a few years ago, mention again that wet dreams are the body's normal way of relieving the testicles when a lot of semen has built up in them. It is one thing to have information about something that will happen one day, and quite another to be reminded of the facts when it occurs. Since your son is apparently feeling anxious about his bodily changes, you will help him to relax; your caring attitude will communicate that you feel his body is just fine. And tell him that he can wait until the next day to do his laundry.

Menstruation

My daughter is twelve and a half, and she has just had her first period. She begged me not to tell her father or anyone else in the family, so I didn't. We have talked about menstruation off and on for several years. One of her friends has had bad cramps, but I assured her that many girls feel just fine throughout their periods, and that if cramps do occur, there are ways they can be relieved or lessened. I thought she was really looking forward to this special event in her body, but she doesn't seem pleased.

Your daughter probably needs some time to adjust to and accept this new change. She is fortunate that you respect her need for a mother-daughter secret. Girls who have been well prepared with the facts about menstruation may still feel terrified when it arrives but ashamed to express their feelings. Some girls become fearful about stains on their clothes, bad odors, or blood running down their legs. To deal with these feelings, they become preoccupied with cleanliness and choose to spend a lot of time alone. No matter how long they have expected and waited for menstruation, they don't feel ready when it arrives.

You need to reassure your daughter that as natural as it is to get a period, it is just as natural not to feel ready for this step into womanhood. Try to alleviate her anxiety by conveying a positive attitude about these new physical changes. Perhaps the two of you could have a secret celebration lunch at a favorite restaurant. Your warm acceptance will help your daughter to accept herself more fully.

The theme of this section has been open communication with children about their bodies. It is important to establish an environment in which children are not afraid to ask questions of an intimate nature or to express their concerns. Honest answers from parents will avoid misconceptions and unnecessary worries.

SELF-PROTECTION

This section considers some key areas of potential danger for children: smoking, drinking, drugs, and sexual abuse. By withholding information and warnings, a parent increases a child's vulnerability. If something terrible happened as a result, it would be hard to forgive oneself for having remained silent. Parents shouldn't give children daily warnings, as the children will soon stop listening. However, warning a child once or twice about such serious issues is not enough; they cannot absorb the information that quickly. At different ages, they will have different questions and concerns. Parents need to decide when to initiate discussions of particular issues.

Drugs

My daughter is seven, and the other day she really scared me. I found her in the kitchen eating vitamins because she likes the flavor. I know she had taken at least a dozen when I found her. Do we need to lock up all of the pills in our house?

It is a good idea to lock up drugs, but most families have their daily vitamins in an easily accessible place. Perhaps you need instead to talk with your daughter about what is safe to eat and what isn't. Explain how some foods help the body while others just fill you up or may do actual harm. Then explain to your daughter that even though one vitamin a day is good for her body, more than that could be really bad, even damaging to her body. Your daughter should be equipped with this information so that she won't feel tempted again.

Smoking and Drinking

Our son is in sixth grade, and his group of friends seems really nice. He has always shown good judgment, but some-

thing happened recently that has us worried. All of these boys were invited to sleep at the home of one of them. The next morning we received a phone call from the boy's mother saying that she was calling every family to report on what happened at the party. It seems these kids got their hands on a pack of cigarettes and some beer. One of the children threw up, and when the parents came in to investigate, they found out what was going on. My husband and I are so furious we want to ground our son, but we can't keep him locked up forever.

Many parents are shocked to learn that some elementary school children experiment with smoking and drinking. These children need adult supervision, but, more importantly, they also need knowledge. Help your son to understand what smoking and drinking can do to harm his body. Let him know that although you understand how strong an influence peer pressure can be, taking good care of his body is more important than being popular.

It is fortunate that this mother called everyone. Perhaps all of the parents and their sons could get together and work out plans to avoid this problem in the future. Each child might feel relieved to know that other parents also oppose smoking and drinking. Through a group effort, you might encourage positive peer pressure.

Incest

My husband and I have eight children and feel good about how much they all seem to enjoy each other's company. We have read and heard about brothers and sisters having sexual relationships with each other, and we can't imagine anything like that happening with our kids. Is there anything we can do to make sure it doesn't?

Bring one of those articles to the family dinner table for a family discussion. Tell the children how badly you feel for the children involved. An open family discussion is an excellent way to let everyone know the ground rules. If one of the children ever sexually approached another family member, this discussion would give the child permission to say no; he or she could remind the other child of the "family ground rules." Be sure to tell your children that they must never let *anyone* convince them to keep a secret about sexual approaches or activities. Even though many parents find this topic difficult to raise, it is far better to take precautions than to have something happen and know you remained silent.

Incest: Warning Signals

Until now, we have never had a problem over my father's living with us. The children have always liked him. My eleven-year-old daughter still does, but she recently confided to me that she doesn't want to be left alone in the house with him. When I tried to talk with her about it, she said that nothing has actually happened but that she feels funny around him and thinks he likes her too much. I remember feeling funny around my father when I was her age. I don't want to look for trouble where there isn't any, but I don't know how to handle this.

Your daughter is lucky that you have that faint memory to help you identify with her feelings. Respect the fact that she doesn't feel safe alone with your father, and make arrangements to avoid this situation. Listening to your daughter's feelings and acting on her wish lets her know that you value her thoughts and that it is safe for her to come to you for help. Basic to your daughter's safety is her ability to communicate openly with you and her knowledge that she can speak up and receive protection.

Incest: Brother and Sister

Several years ago an unfortunate incident occurred in our family: my fourteen-year-old son had sexual relations with his eight-year-old sister. We all went to family counseling, and the therapist had private sessions with my daughter for almost a year. Somehow my daughter just isn't the same. I feel like she doesn't really trust any of us, including her mother and me. I wonder if she'll ever be her old self again.

Fortunately, you did get some professional help, and you probably should have additional sessions. Incest is traumatic for a child, for several reasons. First, children generally trust family members, and incest is a major betrayal of that trust. Second, these encounters often leave children feeling physically hurt and emotionally devastated. Third, children somehow feel responsible and guilty, even though they aren't. It is not surprising that your daughter isn't "the same." It could take a very long time for her to form trusting relationships again. When she is older, she might want to participate in group therapy sessions for incest victims. These groups help each member to know that other people have suffered similarly. Your daughter may well be thinking that she is the only person who has gone through this horrible experience. The continued love and care all of you offer her is basic to her healing.

New Babysitters

Next week my husband and I are going to an all-day party. We are leaving the children in the care of my friend's babysitter. She says the babysitter is reliable, and I trust her judgment. However, my husband and I feel we should say something to the children just in case anything goes wrong. Our kids are friendly and outgoing, and we want to warn them about molesters. At the same time, we don't want to scare them to death or cause them to stop being friendly.

It is possible to remain outgoing and friendly while being alert to and aware of potential danger. Sexual abuse of children occurs more often than anyone would care to believe. One of the frightening aspects of these assaults is that the perpetrators are usually known by the children. Withholding safety warnings increases a child's vulnerability, so occasional reminders are a good idea.

You were wise to select a babysitter your friend uses and trusts. When you have the sitter come over to meet your children, be sure to walk through the house and point out posted lists of family information.

Along with the emergency phone numbers and in-structions regarding meals, bedtimes, and so on, have a list of family safety rules that you and your children compiled.

Family Safety Rules   *We would like to compile a list of family safety rules but don't know where to begin. What should our list include, and how should we go about compiling it?*

You should compile the list as a family, discussing each rule, and the reasons for it, as you are writing it down. And you should review the list from time to time for possible additions. Here are some suggestions to get you started:

☐ Always let a responsible adult know where you are.
☐ If you change plans, call home and let someone know.
☐ If you feel you are in danger, act on it. It is better to be safe than sorry.
☐ Do not get into anyone's car unless your parents have told you it's okay.
☐ If someone asks you to look for a dog or cat, don't go unless your parents approve.
☐ Do not let anyone bribe you with candy, toys, jewelry, money, tickets to a show, or anything else.
☐ Adults don't always use good judgment, and they sometimes do things that are wrong. It is okay to say no and to even yell at an adult if you have to.
☐ If anyone tickles you, pats you, or roughhouses with you and refuses to stop when you ask, stay away from him or her, or get help. People should respect your words and your right to say "stop."
☐ It is wrong for anyone to touch your body if it makes you feel uncomfortable.
☐ Refuse to touch another person's body in any way that makes you feel uncomfortable.
☐ No one has the right to ask you to undress or to undress in front of you.
☐ Always try to use your best judgment.

☐ In new situations, *stop and think.*
☐ If anyone tells you not to tell your parents something because you'll get in trouble, or because it's a secret, don't believe it. *Tell your parents.*
☐ *Taking care of your own body and protecting yourself is one of the most important jobs you have.*

All of the young cousins in our family dread the big family reunions because of one uncle. Whenever the children get within arm's length of him, he grabs them and hugs and kisses them. My son does everything he can to avoid this uncle and shoves the uncle away if he does grab him. I'm sure this uncle is probably harmless and I don't want to encourage my son to be rude, but I'm confused about how to handle the situation.

A Relative Who Makes Children Feel Uncomfortable

This uncle might simply be an affectionate man who is really happy to see his nieces and nephews. His motivation in "grabbing and hugging and kissing" might be totally innocent. Even so, if you force your son to comply, the next adult may not have such innocent motivation when he or she grabs your son. He is not being "rude" by trying to avoid his uncle and by pushing him away if he's grabbed; he is indicating, in an unmistakable way, that he will not be forced to be affectionate. Many parents push their children into kissing a relative or friend in order to be "polite." Do not insist on your child's kissing anyone, and never try to embarrass him into it. There are a lot of ways to be "polite" without kissing. If children are taught and forced to do what adults want them to, how will they resist coercion, bribes, or demands from adults seeking sexual gratification from children?

This uncle's behavior is inappropriate. He is forcing his affection on children. Adult family members should confront him about his behavior and explain that it makes the children uncomfortable. The most important thing you can do is to give your son permission to reject these and any other advances, even if it makes his uncle or some other adult angry.

A Teacher as a Potential Sexual Abuser

Our son has a fifth-grade teacher whom everyone adores. This teacher seems really competent, but my husband and I feel a little concerned because he wants to spend so many out-of-school hours with the boys in his class. First he took them to a movie, then to the park for a picnic, and now he's talking about an overnight camping trip. Doesn't he see enough of these kids at school? Why does he invite the boys and not the girls? We don't want to start any rumors by talking with the other parents, but we think it is odd. When we tried to talk with our son about this, he got really mad. He said we were probably jealous because he likes the teacher so much.

Trust your instincts. You could make other, special plans so that your son will be unable to go on the overnight trip. Another alternative would be for your husband to volunteer to go along. If the teacher's motivation is less than honorable, he won't want another adult with him.

Your son respects and trusts this teacher, so he can't believe that anything could be wrong. Many adults, as well as children, believe that a person with evil intent looks evil. The truth is that many adults with evil intent act very friendly and seem like nice people. Child molesters are a serious danger because they are very patient in establishing close and trusting relationships with children. They often choose careers that will put them in regular contact with children. They make acts like fondling children seem like a natural expression of their love. The truth is, of course, that they love children in unacceptable and harmful ways.

Whether he gets mad or not, you must make your son understand this. Assure him that your motivation is to alert him because you love him. Let him know that you trust his judgment and that you know he will tell you if there are any warning signals. Tell him that we don't always know people as well as we think we do, and that people can change. There is, of course, a good chance that his teacher is innocent. A private family discussion will not harm the teacher, and it could protect your son.

This section covered topics that are upsetting to both parents and children. Self-protection in the areas of drugs, smoking, and drinking often involves resisting peer pressure, which requires inner strength. The possibility of sexual abuse is frightening, but children who are informed, aware, and observant have an edge on danger. A major challenge in parenting is to help children learn to protect themselves.

CONCLUSION

This chapter has discussed ways to help children feel responsible for their own bodies. The pride of caring for one's body can have a positive influence on every facet of a child's life. The child who feels successful in the daily routines at home will enter school and the larger community with self-confidence. This foundation is basic to the process of learning and socialization.

CHAPTER 2

THE SOCIAL AND EMOTIONAL GROWTH OF CHILDREN

Many factors affect the social and emotional growth of children. Parents are the most significant influence on children's feelings about themselves. Children who feel liked and accepted by their parents have a strong foundation for successful social and emotional development.

This chapter will focus on four important areas of social and emotional growth: the effect of personality and behavior on how children are perceived by others; moral development as it relates to family and friends; children's fears, which can both hamper their emotional growth and protect them; and friendship, which children often identify as the most important part of their lives. The suggestions offer ways for parents to foster healthy social and emotional growth in children.

PERSONALITY AND BEHAVIOR

Controversy continues as to how much of a child's personality is determined by heredity, and how much by environmental influences. Watching newborn infants, one quickly becomes aware of the temperamental variations among children. From the beginning of life, the infants' varying energy levels and abilities to respond to sound, touch, and visual stimuli offer clues to their emerging personalities.

Parents are the most important influence on a child's emerging personality. A young child's primary contact with the world is through the family. Children learn to view themselves through their parents' reactions to their behavior.

Children test out different kinds of behavior on the people close to them, imitating other children, adults, and characters they see on TV or read about in books. How parents respond to these behavioral experiments affects their child's personality development. Calm and caring reactions within a supportive environment can help children to learn socially acceptable standards of behavior.

Each child has a unique way of interacting in the world. It is important to observe a child in many different situations; a child's reaction in one setting might differ from the same child's reaction in another setting. It is the child's *typical* conduct that helps us to understand his or her developing personality. For example, if a child whines a few times a week to get a desired response, the whining is probably no cause for concern; but if a child whines a number of times every day, he or she might have learned that whining causes adults to give in to his or her wishes. When a behavorial response is predictable in many situations, people begin to describe the child's personality in terms of the behavior. If parents can recognize an unwanted form of behavior in its early stages, they can try to redirect or alter it before it becomes a personality characteristic.

Some potentially annoying forms of behavior are described in the following section. Without parental intervention, these forms of behavior could become personality characteristics. The suggestions offer a variety of ways to intervene and attempt to alter the child's behavior. The goal is to help children develop personality characteristics that will make them feel worthwhile.

Imitation

I feel upset when I hear my four-year-old daughter imitate me. She uses exactly my tone of voice to yell at her dolls or friends. Before she was born I was determined to be the best parent I could possibly be. When I see and hear her copying my worst behavior, I feel like a failure. How can I get her to copy my best, not my worst, behavior?

It is only natural for your daughter to imitate you. She cannot be expected to imitate only your good behavior; in fact, she probably thinks that any behavior you display is appropriate behavior. So you must work to change those aspects of your behavior that bother you when you see them appearing in her. Tell the whole family that you are going to work on changing your behavior. Plan how to stop yourself once you start yelling. Also, plan ways to express your anger in an acceptable manner. Ask your daughter to help you change this pattern by telling you when she hears you yelling. Your determination and thoughtful planning will help you to implement any behavioral changes you desire. Sharing your goal and the process for reaching it will provide an excellent learning experience for your daughter.

Acting Like a Baby

Last month I returned to work after spending the first six and a half years of my daughter's life at home. My daughter has always seemed advanced, and her behavior has been excellent. Suddenly, she has begun to act like a baby both at home and at school. She now asks me to do things that I know she is perfectly capable of doing herself. Yesterday, for example, she asked me to tie her shoes, even though she has been tying them herself for a long time. The only thing that has changed in her life is my working. We need the money, and I like my job. For these reasons, the problem cannot be solved by my quitting work.

It is fortunate that your daughter has found a way to communicate her feelings. Undoubtedly, your job has upset her and she is acting like a younger child in a plea for your attention and help. The problem with this inappropriate form of self-assertion is that parents, peers, and teachers usually reject babyish behavior, compounding the child's problem.

There are several things you might try to stop this behavior and to help your daughter feel secure again. Find a small amount of time, as little as fifteen minutes, when the two of you can be together every day without interruption. Occasionally, it could help to let her pretend she is your baby during these few minutes together. Show her how you took care of her and tell her what she was like as a baby. During the rest of the day, request and expect six-year-old behavior.

Be sure to compliment your daughter when she does act her age. Search for ways to involve her in your new job and, if possible, let her visit your place of work. If you can't have her visit, bring home photographs of the job site. Ask her to draw a picture that you can show your friends at work. Tell her what you like and dislike about the job. Explain how this job is economically helping the family and tell her how happy you feel when you get your paychecks. If possible, bring a simple task home and let your daughter help you with it.

She might feel a lot better just knowing more about your work and participating in small ways. Your new job is perceived as a real threat to her emotional security. She needs to be assured in many different ways that your special bond will continue even though you are working.

Selfishness

My wife and I hate to admit that our son is an unpleasant person to be around. He is eight years old and very selfish, and we are afraid that he will never change. At dinner one night, he mentioned that no one at school likes him. He pretends that he doesn't care, but we know that he does. We are afraid to think that he might be like this all his life.

Your son wouldn't mention his classmates' dislike of him if it didn't bother him. If he wants to change, he certainly can. People can modify and change their behavior throughout life. Parents may be tempted to feel disappointed in their childrens' behavior and to nag and complain about it. It is critical not to fall into this pattern but to help your son identify alternatives to his behavior.

You might try having a family discussion to help your son gain insight into his behavior and then make a plan to change it. During this discussion, select any four people outside of your family unit whom you all really like. Help each other to make a list of the things you like most about them. Discuss and examine the personality characteristics that appear on this list. Talk about the ways in which these favorite people are alike and the ways in which they differ. Pick several characteristics all of you admire in these four people and agree among yourselves to imitate these characteristics during the coming week. Then have another meeting to discuss how people reacted to each of you. By having the whole family participate in this plan, you won't cause your son to feel that he is being picked on. Be sure to compliment each other on the experiments that brought favorable responses. The very act of recognizing and praising positive interactions tends to increase their occurrence. Before long, you might see some dramatic, positive shifts in your son's human-relation skills.

Lack of Appreciation

I was terribly embarrassed at my daughter's seventh birthday party. She opened her gifts at a fast pace and hardly took the time to look at any of them. It was obvious that she favored a stuffed animal and disliked all the clothes. I didn't know what to say or do.

Your daughter was probably unaware that her feelings were obvious. There are many ways to approach this situation, both directly and indirectly.

You might tell your daughter that several of the party guests looked sad because she didn't seem to like their gifts. At another time, ask her how she feels when friends open her gifts. Another approach is to find someone who can serve as a positive example— a friend or relative (it can be an adult or a child) who always expresses joy and appreciation upon receiving a gift. Arrange for your daughter to attend an event where this person will receive a gift; by seeing how appreciative behavior brings pleasure to all, your daughter may decide to try it herself the next time she receives something.

A suggestion for the next party is to avoid having the opening of gifts be a formal part of the occasion; instead, have your daughter open each one as her guests arrive. For some children it is less intimidating to open gifts without the entire group watching. Also, in a one-to-one situation, she will be unable to simply skip over a present she doesn't particularly like.

Our son is nine years old, and just about everything he says is sarcastic or insulting. I think it is meant in fun, but sometimes I can't tell his real intention. I think he could hurt someone's feelings without meaning to. We used to have normal conversations; I don't understand why he now needs to be this way.

Sarcasm

If your son has become increasingly sarcastic in his interactions with family members, he may be concerned about his independence or individuality. He could be trying out different personality traits.

As your son approaches adolescence, he is trying to show control. Sarcastic remarks or insults delivered in a playful context can be used to assert power, especially over an authority figure. This seems to be a way to deal with conflicts or hostile feelings without appearing to hurt anyone intentionally. Your son probably feels he can get away with comments he ordinarily might be reprimanded for when he disguises them with humor. If he goes too far, he can reduce their offensiveness by claiming that he was "just kidding." At the same time, the child can put the offended listener on the defensive by questioning that person's ability to "take a joke." In a sense, he is able to hide behind his joking. Whatever his purpose is, he is experiencing a sense of control.

If your son's sarcasm hurts your feelings, let him know. At times you might ask, "Are you serious or just kidding?" Remember that finding humorous ways to deal with some of life's serious issues is an excellent way to cope. Your honest reactions will help your son differentiate between good humor and cutting sarcasm.

My son was a part of a group of girls and boys who decided to have some fun with a neighbor's house when its owners were out of town. Included in their mischief was throwing toilet paper in the trees, rubbing soap on the windows, and ripping plants out of the garden. The group was caught, and the parents met to figure out what the youngsters could do to make up for the damage. The children did not have

Excessive Guilt

*enough money to cover the damage involved. They agreed
to do yard work for the neighbors every weekend for two
months. My son goes right over there every Saturday to
do his work, but he still feels terrible about what happened.
I wonder how long this guilt will last. I feel that it is time
for him to get on with his life and let bygones be bygones.*

The weekend yard work probably serves as a continual
reminder to your son of what happened, keeping the
incident fresh in his mind. It is healthy for him to feel
remorse; he intentionally harmed someone's property,
and expressing guilt indicates that he knows right from
wrong.

Help your son to understand that there are several
ways to forgive himself. One is by doing yard work
to clean up the harmed property. The next important
step is to avoid making a similar mistake in the future.
When the work is completed and when he feels confident that he will be able to control his future behavior, he will probably feel better.

Parents are their children's most important role models. They need to
display the kind of behavior they want their children to learn.

Children are often close observers of incidents that parents might consider inconsequential. For example, think of the husband who calls to his
wife as she reaches to answer the telephone, "If that's Joe, tell him I'm
not at home." The wife follows these directions and tells Joe her husband
is out. The children have witnessed both parents in a lie. Children learn
to be honest or dishonest through observing their parents' actions and
words. A child who respects his or her parents—and feels respected by
them—has an important foundation for positive behavior.

There is a danger in placing too great an emphasis on the aspects of
a child's personality that annoy the parents. When this occurs, children
undoubtedly receive too much attention for inappropriate ways of acting,
and such incidents increase. Parents need to spend more time and energy
focusing on the kind of behavior that they want to encourage.

Human beings have a wonderful potential for change. Personality does
not have to remain static; at any age, parents and children can continue
to grow, change, and improve their personalities. Parents can take a dy-
namic part in their children's personality development. They can offer
suggestions for change, both helping children to modify or eradicate undesirable behavior and encouraging desirable behavior.

MORAL DEVELOPMENT

Moral development is an ongoing process. Children do not suddenly acquire a sense of right and wrong; it develops over a period of years. Young children usually try to do what their parents expect, to please them or avoid punishment. Parents should help children develop their *own* decision-making powers and internal controls.

A child must learn to recognize morally acceptable standards of behavior and learn to live comfortably within the boundaries established by these standards. From this recognition comes the challenge of resisting temptation, controlling impulses, and making sound decisions before acting. The following examples illustrate some of the moral dilemmas that children and their parents face.

Stealing

My five-year-old son has developed the habit of returning home from friends' houses with one or more small toys tucked in his pocket. When I ask him about these toys, he claims that they are his or that he accidentally took them. Should I make more of an issue of his stealing? I know it's important, but I don't know how to handle it.

It is not unusual for young children to lie in order to avoid possible punishment. They often have trouble remembering what is really true as they begin to believe their own lies.

Parents can avoid a lot of lies by making statements instead of asking questions. If a parent says, "Did you steal your friend's truck?" the child will probably deny it. Instead, the parent might say, "Let's talk about taking that truck back to your friend." Briefly discuss how your son would feel if someone took his toys. Help him return the toy without being punitive or trying to embarrass him. Be firm about the fact that the toy belongs with its rightful owner.

Anticipate that a similar situation will occur in the future and plan ways to handle it and encourage self-control. Offer your son some alternatives to stealing; he might ask to borrow a toy he really likes, trade toys with a friend for a few days, or begin a wish list of toys he would like to buy. Long lectures usually result in children's tuning out their parents. It is wiser to deal with only a few points at a time. The most important concept to communicate to your child is how proud he'll feel when he really wants something and doesn't allow himself to take it. This impulse control is the beginning of self-discipline and contributes to a child's self-respect.

**Imaginary
Scapegoats**

Our six-year-old daughter has quite an imagination. Unfortunately, she often uses it to try to get out of trouble. For example, the other day my wife asked her why the brand-new tube of toothpaste was empty. She said a giant lizard used the whole thing to clean his huge teeth. We think she is old enough to admit what she has done instead of blaming an imaginary lizard.

Your daughter is testing the boundaries of make-believe. You need to help her learn the difference between appropriate and inappropriate times for using her imagination. It seems easier to blame someone else when things go wrong; she must learn to take the consequences for her own actions. Tell her to save her lizard stories for a make-believe story time and to tell you how *she* used all of the toothpaste so fast.

Lying

I have always had a very close relationship with my daughter, but during the last few weeks I have caught her in several lies. It breaks my heart. Since we are so close, I can't figure out why she would lie to me. The things she lied about were really unimportant.

The most important clue in your comments is the close bond between you and your daughter. Perhaps her "unimportant lies" are a way of trying to experience some independence from you. Sometimes children lie specifically to see if they can keep a secret from their parents. Chances are that this phase will swiftly pass. Try to refrain from searching for lies; that serves only to induce excessive guilt. Buy your daughter a diary that locks, and respect her need to have secrets and to be separate. It is wonderful for children and parents to be close, but it is also important for children to know that they can function successfully on their own.

I don't know what to do about my son, who is eight. He **Rigid about Rules**
enjoys spending hours with his friends. The catch is that everyone has to play by the rules. If one member of the group disagrees with or tries to vary any of the rules, my son gets frantic. He will quit the game before he'll bend a rule even slightly.

Your son is passing through a very normal stage of moral development. Between seven and nine years of age, it is common for children to take the rules of a game very seriously. When this happens, the rules can become overly rigid. It might help you to recognize the importance of this stage. Children who learn to play by the rules are in the process of accepting society's rules.

Young children are first taught to comply with family rules and expectations. Then they attend school and are expected to follow their classroom and school rules. Your son is in the midst of expanding the rules printed on a game box or handed down by parents or older children.

At approximately ten years of age, children begin to change their attitudes about rules and acquire a sense of cooperation. They begin to negotiate and compromise. It might be helpful to point out to your son that his attitude about rules has disrupted many games. Discuss with him what could be done to avoid future conflicts. It might help to post the rules and go over them at the beginning of a game. If the group cannot agree on the rules, it might be better to select another game.

Our son spends a lot of time with one group of classmates. **Bad Companions**
One of the boys was suspended for cheating during a test. While I was still feeling upset about this incident, my son

confided in me about another one: my son and his friends all sneaked in the side door of a movie theater last week. I'm disturbed by the bad influence of these boys. I don't want my son to be an outcast, but the idea of cheating in school and sneaking into a movie theater really scares me.

Be sure to tell your son how glad you are that he trusted you with the information about sneaking into the movie theater. He undoubtedly told you because he felt guilty about this act. Praise him for knowing right from wrong. Expressing guilt usually means that moral development is in progress. Help him to think of alternatives should a similar situation arise.

You want your son to experience the feelings of self-worth that come from resisting temptation. Peer pressure can be very powerful. Help your son to realize that if a group rejects him because of his standards, it might be time to find new friends. Respecting oneself is more important than submitting to group pressure.

Teaching Morality

My husband continually gives lectures to our children about how and why they should live a moral life. I have watched the children give each other glances of disgust. I have heard them moan, "Oh, no, not another sermon." I can tell that they count the minutes until he finishes. I'm sure this can't be an effective way to teach morality, but I haven't come up with a better approach.

A game is one way to approach the subject of moral values without being preachy. For example, write descriptions on cards of different situations that pose moral dilemmas. Make sure you include some of the issues your children have faced or will have to face. Place the cards upside down in the center of the family circle. Each member will take a turn to draw a card and try to think of solutions to the problem stated. Do not inhibit anyone by saying that his or her answer is wrong. When you eventually draw the same card, everyone will have a chance to hear how you would solve the problem.

This game would help your children understand that there are a number of ways to solve any given problem. It would also give your husband the opportunity to effectively express his opinion on a topic he values.

Guiding children in moral development is closely related to the subject of discipline, discussed in Chapter 7 of this book. The ultimate goal of parental discipline is self-discipline, which is the foundation for moral development. It is essential that parents believe that their children are worthy human beings—and communicate that belief to them. Children who feel good about themselves have a strong foundation from which to make the many moral decisions that will face them throughout their entire lifetime.

FEAR

Fear is a normal part of growing up. Children share many of the same fears. Some of these fears change and then disappear with growth. Ideally, children retain the healthy fears that protect them from danger, but not irrational and unproductive fears. Parents are the key influence on how children deal with fear; they can intensify or alleviate children's fears through their reactions. Fearful parents may raise children so fearful that they feel anxious and powerless. Such children learn to distrust people and things in their environment, viewing the world as a dangerous place. Fears that are too intense and too prolonged can harm the developing personality.

Parents who grew up with many fears and continue to be troubled by them may want to seek professional help in this area of parenting. Through learning how to help their children overcome fear, the parents will learn to cope more effectively themselves. Children who learn how to face and conquer their fears feel powerful, rather than threatened and helpless.

Overly protective parents seem preoccupied with fears related to their children's safety, imagining many dangerous possibilities. Consequently, they continue to protect their children long after the children should have learned to protect themselves. The parents remain in full charge. An example of such protective tendencies might be refusal to let a child participate in sports or any other potentially dangerous activity. Such parents continually voice warnings and monitor all of their children's activities, purportedly for safety reasons. These children will probably lack the confidence essential for success in the world, depending completely on their parents, who always watch out for them. Eventually, some of these children might demand the chance to grow. They might even secretly seek out forbidden activities to assert their independence and thus learn to rely on their own judgment.

How fortunate are the children who feel safe and protected while they are small but learn to take care of themselves as they grow. Their parents believe that their children can and will use good judgment and know how to protect themselves or get help when necessary. This belief is transmitted to the children, often simply by the parents' attitude, and the children grow up with an inner assurance that they will succeed in the world.

Some of the fears children face are relatively simple for parents to deal with. For example, a child who is afraid of a vacuum cleaner's noise could be put in charge of the switch. The child's control over the feared noise should make it less frightening. Children do need to be able to differentiate between realistic and unrealistic fears. If parents anxiously cater to every tiny fear a child experiences, the child will be unable to recognize a genuinely dangerous situation. A three-year-old might appear equally afraid of a windup toy scurrying across the floor and a strange dog growling and baring its teeth. It would be inappropriate for the parent to react in similar ways to these situations. The parent might get down on the floor and reach for the windup toy to demonstrate its harmlessness. With the dog, however, the parent would praise the child for recognizing its anger and avoiding potential danger. The child needs to learn to tell the difference between a harmless situation and a dangerous one, and the parents' reactions will help the child to see that some fears are healthy while others are groundless.

The following section offers examples of children's typical fears and suggests ways to help children conquer them.

Nightmares

I don't know what to do about my son's scary dreams. He wants to avoid going to sleep so that he won't have to experience another nightmare. When I turn his lights out, he actually starts to tremble.

If grown-ups could recall the terror of childhood nightmares, it would help them to understand what their children are going through. Some children actually wake up screaming and sweating because their nightmares seem so real.

The first step is to examine your child's daily routine. Could anything new be prompting these nightmares? Be sure to ask him about what is going on during the day. Nightmares can serve as warning signals for parents. When a specific source of anxiety is identified, a plan to alter or remove it can be initiated.

Sometimes, though, there isn't an obvious cause for children's nightmares. Then parents must focus on reducing tension at bedtime. You might work on associating the darkness at bedtime with something pleasant. Sing songs together or listen to relaxing music. Your son might need to sleep with the light on for a while. Tell him that he can turn the light off himself when he feels ready. Some children are satisfied to sleep with a flashlight within reach. The point is to give them control over the darkness.

Children who are experiencing nightmares usually disrupt their parents' sleep and express fear over staying alone in their rooms. To break this pattern, it could help for a parent to spend a few nights in the child's room. Some children respond to simply having a stuffed animal assigned to guard their bed at night. Point out to your son that he is already doing a good job of stopping scary dreams by waking up. Suggest that, when he awakens, he give his stuffed animal a big hug and even turn on his light for a minute or so to reassure himself that he's in familiar, unthreatening surroundings. Once he realizes that a frightening dream will disappear as soon as he wakes up, he may be able to make himself awaken as soon as it begins.

Another approach to scary dreams is to act out the situations they present. If, for example, he dreams of a monster, ask him what he would like to have happen to the monster. Using a stuffed animal or clay figure, have him demonstrate what he means; he will, of course, defeat the monster, giving him a feeling of power. Before he goes to sleep at night, tell him to try to change the dream—to make it come out the way *he* wants it to—if it occurs again. Many children stop having particular scary dreams once they have acted them out during the day. Other children have reported actually changing dreams while they remained asleep.

It is important for parents to help children gain a sense of mastery over dreams. The solutions suggested here, once implemented, do not depend on parents for stopping scary dreams and they present one more opportunity for helping children gain a sense of personal power.

Separation

My daughter is going to begin kindergarten in two months. She says she will not go to school unless I go with her. We have always been close, and I have rarely left her with a babysitter. I can tell that she really is afraid about being away from me at school. Is there any way that I can help to make this separation easier for her?

Going to school does mean hours of being away from you. Anxiety over such separation is common in children. There are a few ways you might help your daughter reduce her fears and have an easier transition into school.

During the next two months it would be wise to accustom your daughter to being away from you. Carefully select a good babysitter or a caring relative and arrange for this person to spend some time with your daughter every week. At first you could stay with them. Once your daughter is comfortable with this person, leave them for short periods, then gradually longer periods. Always be truthful with your daughter about how soon you are going to return. Call her if you are going to be late. Her ability to conquer her fear of separation greatly depends on her being able to trust what you say. Be sure to convey your confidence about the separation. Tell her that you know what great company she'll be for the person taking care of her. Explain that when you return you'll talk with each other about the things you did. If she tells you that she is going to cry or that she did cry, let her know that it is fine to express her feelings through tears and that you know her sadness is only temporary.

The two months of short separations will help your daughter prepare for the daily separation of kindergarten. You might also attempt to find another neighborhood child who will begin kindergarten at the same time. Arrange for your daughter and this child to play together several times before school begins. Perhaps they could go to school together on the first day. It would help your daughter to have a familiar face in her classroom.

The anxiety caused by separation from parents is sometimes compounded by fears of getting lost in the school building. Ask for permission to visit the school and walk around with your daughter. Locate the classroom, the main office, the bathroom, the library, the drinking fountain, and the playground. Have your daughter lead you back to "her room" from all the different locations. This will help her become oriented to the building.

Taking photographs might be another way to help your daughter become familiar with the school while she is still feeling safe in her own home. Photographs of the play equipment in the classroom and on the play yard will give the two of you a chance to talk about some of the things she will be doing. Be sure she knows exactly where you will be waiting for her when school ends each day.

Although you will not want kindergarten to be the only topic of conversation during the next two months, you should accept your daughter's feelings and acknowledge that kindergarten is a big, scary, and exciting step. You might want to drop a note to the teacher shortly before school begins; alerting her to your child's anxiety could prompt a little added attention during the first few days.

Some children are comforted during separations by carrying in their pocket a small item—a handkerchief or a barrette, for example—that belongs to their mother. You might surprise your daughter with a little drawing in her lunch bag. Let her know what you two are going to do after school so that she can be looking forward to it. Your sensitivity and careful planning will undoubtedly make the transition easier for both of you.

Animals

We recently gave our daughter a kitten for her third birthday. We kept telling our five-year-old son to treat it gently, but he didn't listen, and a few days ago it gave him a nasty scratch on the face. This kitten has never scratched our daughter, who is gentle with it. Now our son seems constantly nervous about the kitten. He shrieks whenever it approaches. Since we intend to keep the kitten, is there any way we can quickly eradicate this fear?

Your son's fear is reasonable even though he helped to cause the scratch. His fear is obviously intense and probably cannot be "quickly" removed. A gradual approach, however, will probably succeed.

Since your son is a more important member of your family than the kitten, restrict the kitten to certain rooms. This will give your son a chance to relax without constantly worrying about its presence; if he doesn't feel protected, he will have trouble listening to your explanation of why the kitten scratched him.

Kissing and comforting your son during his terrified outbursts would only reinforce his fear. Teasing or ridiculing him for being nervous about a tiny kitten would intensify his feelings of shame and self-doubt. Your job is to help him relax and learn safe ways to play with animals.

Take time to help your son become comfortable with the kitten. Talk about some of the kitten's pleasant features, such as its soft fur, sparkling eyes, and long whiskers. From a safe distance, let your son observe you playing with it. It is important for him to see how to be gentle, rather than just be told. You might let him help tie a bell to the end of a long strand of yarn for the kitten to chase. Explain that you want the yarn long enough so that you won't get scratched when the kitten swats at the bell. Slowly let your son become reacquainted with the kitten. Eventually he might request a pet of his own.

Drowning

When we all went to the beach last week, our six-year-old daughter was tossed over by a wave. She left the water the minute she got on her feet, and she cried for a long time. She says she will never go swimming again, and I know she really means it. My husband told her that she will swim again and that he is going to take her right into the water the next time we go to the beach. He thinks that by proving to her that she can swim again he'll take away her fear. I'm not convinced that this is a good approach. Is there another way to get her back in the water?

If your husband forces your daughter into the ocean, she probably will not lose her fear of the water and she undoubtedly will lose trust in her own father. His imposing his will on her could actually increase her fear. The waves made her feel out of control, and that helplessness would be compounded by her father. To control her fear, it is imperative that she feel in control of herself.

Encourage your daughter to talk about what happened. Explain how powerful some waves are and describe what an undercurrent is. Agree that being unexpectedly knocked over is scary, even for adults. Remind her about the great way she took charge and stood up between the waves. Describe how quickly and safely she moved herself right out of the water. Her tears let the family know how scared she was. Talk about how wise it is to stay out of the water when the waves are too strong. A healthy respect for the ocean's potential danger is important.

Initially it might be helpful to let her experience being in calmer water. Having a good time in a swimming pool or a lake will remind her that she really does enjoy the water. When you do return to the ocean, assure her that she'll go in when she feels ready. You might join her in building sand castles and looking for shells at the water's edge. You could play tag, darting in and out of the water. Let her observe the rest of you conquering the waves, and before long she will probably be able to join you.

Scary Movies

Our neighbors do not monitor what their children watch on TV. Our six-year-old son was playing at their house once when they watched a monster movie. He came home crying, and ever since he's been panicky about monsters in his room at bedtime. He recently found out that the same movie is going to be shown every week for the next month, and he wants to see it again. Since it frightened him so much the first time, I think that would be a mistake. Why would he even want to put himself through those fears again?

When children repeatedly view something that is scary, they make themselves less sensitive to it. Your son probably wants to conquer his fear of this movie monster. Some children recreate scary movies by talking out the frightening episodes over and over again. This verbal repetition helps them to feel in control of their fear.

It is not advisable to expose children to movies that will scare them. They will have enough fears to conquer during childhood as it is. However, your son has already seen the movie, so it is already in his mind. Because he wants to see it again, arrange to watch it with him. During intermission or after the movie, talk about ways you might have saved yourselves from the monster. Children enjoy imagining themselves slaying the feared monster and safely escaping.

Some children insist on checking their rooms for lurking monsters before they feel safe enough to get into bed. If your son requests this kind of search, help him and reassure him that he is safe. He might want to ring a loud bell in his room to chase away potential monsters. This represents another way to take charge of the environment.

No matter how absurd your son's fears might seem to you, refrain from ridicule or laughing. He needs to express his fears in order to control them. If he feels ashamed of his fears, he might keep them secret, which could make them more intense.

Nuclear War

Our son has begun to worry continually about being blown up in a nuclear war. We rarely discuss this topic, so we can't figure out why he is obsessed with it. One of his third-grade classmates has expressed the same fear, and all of their play is about the world blowing up. We really don't know what to do.

Nuclear warfare is a difficult topic for many parents to discuss because it arouses fear. However, acknowledging fear usually makes it more manageable. Even though you and your husband rarely discuss this topic, it has become a real issue in your son's life. You certainly don't want him to dwell on this or any other frightening possibility, but since his fear is not momentary, you will need to deal with it in order to ease his anxiety.

First, find out where he has gathered his information and find out more about his beliefs. Many children learn about world problems by watching TV. At times they misinterpret what they see and hear. Knowing what is already in your son's head will help you understand his obsession, even though it won't eradicate it.

Having a classmate that shares his feelings probably assures your son that there isn't something wrong with him. Help these children find constructive ways to deal with their feelings. Perhaps their teacher will let them work together on a report for their class. This would give them the opportunity to gather some accurate information. A homemade film or drawings could depict the difference between war and peace. You and their teacher might help them think of ways to live more peacefully both at home and in the classroom. Some children have written letters to friends, relatives, or world leaders, offering constructive suggestions for world peace.

Any of these activities will help shift your son's focus from disaster to hope. We certainly want to encourage future generations to make the world a better place.

Death

My mother lived with us until she died a year ago. From time to time, my wife and I try unsuccessfully to talk with our eight-year-old daughter about her grandmother, with whom she was very close. We can't figure out why our daughter refuses to discuss the subject. Another thing we have noticed during this last year is her fearfulness when my wife and I leave for a weekend or even for an evening. She asks a lot of questions about where we will be and what time we'll be home.

Many children delay grieving until they are older and feel more capable of handling their emotions. It is important to continue mentioning your mother occasionally during conversations. This will share your mourning process and memories with your daughter. You might want to fill a small box with some special treasures that belonged to your mother. Once in a while, show your daughter some of the trinkets and talk about the recollections they hold for you. Before long she might join in and ask you a few questions, and eventually she might volunteer some of her own memories.

As you implied, your daughter's anxiety about your leaving her is undoubtedly related to your mother's death. She lost her grandmother, and now she probably fears losing the most important adults in her life. You need to be very open with your daughter about this. Tell her that you cannot promise her that you won't die, but that at your age the odds are very much against it.

Some children want and need to know what will happen to them if their parents die. If your daughter asks, explain to her the careful provisions you and your wife have made for her in case something happens to you. Tell her why you feel the people you have picked as guardians would take very good care of her. But reassure her that these provisions are unlikely to be needed.

Lack of Fears

What can I do about a child who is fearless? Our daughter is willing to try any new challenge or adventure. She has needed stitches because of accidents at home and at school. We appreciate her spirited nature, but we have become increasingly worried about her physical safety.

It is lucky for the world that some children seek out challenging adventures as they grow up. Some of them probably grow up to be adults who break sports records or orbit the earth in spaceships. Taking risks in life can be productive and exciting. But, as you pointed out, it can also prove physically harmful.

Your task is to help your daughter learn how to take good care of her body while taking risks. Thinking before acting can avert accidents without lessening your daughter's fun. You might want to write a simple story about her past adventures. Describe incidents where she succeeded without injury as well as the accidents that did occur. Together, search for ideas about how she could have avoided the accidents. Help her to think ahead about some future adventures in which she'll find ways to avoid injury and still have fun. Your daughter needs to be shown how to take care of herself and be given the responsibility for doing so.

We cannot and should not try to raise children who are completely free of fear. Fear is a necessary part of self-preservation. We need, however, to help children differentiate between realistic and unrealistic fears. Children's fears range from fears of specific events to fears of imagined situations that could not really occur. They struggle to conquer imaginary monsters and fears of the night. Whatever fear a child is working on, parents must help the child find the inner strength to work it out. Such children learn to cope with the world as self-reliant human beings and to feel safe even without their parents.

Children need self-confidence to handle the problems of childhood effectively. As they acquire this confidence, many of their fears will fade or dissipate. We don't want children to be recklessly brave, but neither do we want them to be immobilized by fears. Children need to recognize and maintain healthy, realistic fears and develop a sense of basic trust, coping mechanisms, and the self-confidence to move out and conquer their world.

FRIENDSHIP

Friends are an important aspect of everyone's life. They can be a source of both pleasure and frustration. Friends enable children to have experiences with others outside their family circle. Through these experiences, children learn the ingredients of successful friendships.

Parents cannot make friends for their children, but they can provide opportunities for friendships to develop. Understanding the important role of friends in a child's growth and development helps parents to encourage friendships. For many children, friends are more important than schoolwork, hobbies, sports, or other activities. The following concerns have been raised by parents who want to help their children develop social skills.

The pediatrician encouraged me to send my son to nursery school. She felt it would give him the chance to play with   **Nursery School Playmates** *children his own age. I have watched my son at school and have noticed that he really does not play with the other children. When we are on the way to school he often talks about a special friend of his, but he doesn't seem to relate to this supposed friend, or anyone else, when they are together.*

Many children of nursery school age anticipate seeing favorite people when they get to school. Thinking about these people helps reduce the stress of separation from parents.

Also, young children frequently prefer to play near each other, rather than directly with each other. Children learn from observing each other. This is called "parallel play." Your son is certainly aware of the presence of peers, even though he may choose to act as if he is alone. It is important for you to let him enjoy and experience nursery school in the way most comfortable for him.

Imaginary Friends *I feel concerned about my son because he has imaginary friends. He seems perfectly content to spend all afternoon playing with them. He talks about these "friends," sometimes describing complicated situations involving them. Is this normal behavior for a four-year-old?*

Many normal, healthy children converse with imaginary friends. These "friends" are always available, provide a captive audience, and never tell a child what to do. Having such imaginary friends allows a child to be the "boss" of another "person." Children can learn a lot from these relationships. Even though the friends are imaginary, conflicts can be resolved and fearful ideas explored and defused.

It is important for your child to realize the difference between real and imaginary friends. Provide opportunities for him to play with other children. Through real friends, your son can learn the give-and-take of relationships. As respectful parents, however, you should accept your child's imaginary friends as well as his real friends.

My six-year-old daughter has a friend who is nice to her one minute and mean to her the next. There is no obvious reason for this sudden shift in behavior. Sometimes the girls play beautifully, but it is difficult to predict when things will change. I find this situation disturbing, because when the mood suddenly changes, my daughter often ends up in tears.

Difficult Playmates

It is important for you to respect your daughter's choice of friends, but, at the same time, you should share with her your observations and feelings. Explain to your daughter how upsetting it is for you when her friend gets in these moods. Tell her that you feel both angry and sad because of the many times she has ended up crying. Mention that you have not seen her crying when she plays with other friends. Encourage your daughter to play with this friend less frequently; she needs to experience friendships that do not cause so many "bad" feelings.

One month ago our family moved. We timed our move so that our daughter could start third grade at the beginning of the school year. She has not seemed happy during the whole first month of classes. She used to enjoy school and was happy when she came home. Now, she mopes around the house saying she doesn't have any friends. We are wondering what we might do to help her.

Making Friends

Let your daughter know that you recognize how she is feeling and that moving is difficult. Leaving old friends is hard and finding new ones is often harder. Offer to discuss ways to make new friends. Together you could probably create a list of suggestions, which might include some of the following ideas:

- [ ] Ask the teacher if there are any other third-grade girls just entering the school.
- [ ] Find out if there are any after-school programs for third-graders.
- [ ] Invite classmates or neighbors to come over for a visit.
- [ ] Plan a party and invite all of the third-graders.

Remind your daughter that it takes time to make friends. Your support and advice during this time may help her not to feel so alone.

Cross-age Friendship

Our son seems to choose friends who are older. We are concerned because we feel he should also have friends his own age. Would it be meddling to discuss our feelings about this?

If you have strong feelings about any area of your child's development, it is not meddling to raise the issue. But while you encourage your son to find some friends his own age, be sure to compliment him on having successfully maintained friendships with his older friends.

Friends of diverse ages and abilities can provide rich experiences for children. They allow children to experience themselves as leaders and followers, as winners and losers, and as equals. Sometimes younger children select older friends to reduce the stress caused by competing with equals in age or ability; an older friend could give a child an excuse for being the loser in a competitive situation. But age should not be a sole factor in determining friendships. Mutual respect between friends is far more important.

Forgiving and Forgetting

The other night my daughter and her neighborhood friends were playing hide-and-seek. One of the girls encouraged all of the others to hide from my daughter. She came home in tears and said she would never play with that girl again. Since that incident, the girls have resolved their differences and everything seems to be fine. The problem is that I am still angry and feel that I do not want this little girl to come to our house. I think she would be a negative influence on my daughter.

Children need to learn the negative aspects of friendships, as well as the positive ones. If children stopped seeing everyone with whom they had a disagreement, they might not have any friends at all.

It is fine for your daughter to be angry and to communicate her feelings. It sounds as if your daughter is also able to forget past anger and live in the present.

Your grudge is not a good example for your daughter. She may be able to teach you a lesson in this instance. Do not fight her battles. Rather, learn from her maturity. It seems that the problem is no longer a problem for her.

Groups, Clubs, Cliques

My eleven-year-old son has become involved with a group of boys that get together constantly and have formed a sort of club. He says that everyone in the club has to dress alike and get similar haircuts. I feel like my son has lost his individuality and I worry about the possibility of his getting into some kind of trouble. He used to enjoy doing things with the family, but now he wants to spend all of his time with his club friends. Should I try to get him away from them?

Many children go through a phase of wanting to belong to a club. As long as you feel the club's activities are acceptable, do not interfere. If your son's schoolwork suffers, or if you feel he is compromising his values, then speak up. When parents recognize that their children are on the verge of questionable activities, they need to intervene. Groups of close friends provide opportunities not available in individual friendships. The group can carry out activities that several friends would not attempt. Groups allow children to feel both that they are similar to their peers and that they are special. Clothing and fads are harmless ways in which group members show that they are alike. Cooperative efforts can be learned from being part of a close-knit group. Since few children seem to feel really popular with their peers, it is fortunate that most children have the chance to experience the comfort and support of belonging to a group.

Friends with Differing Interests

Our daughter is upset because her two best friends have become "boy crazy." They spend all of their time talking about boys and making up schemes that will allow them to "accidentally" encounter boys. Our daughter is not as interested in boys as her friends are, but she considers it necessary to go along with their plans for the sake of friendship.

This is a classic example of peer pressure. Your daughter feels that her friendship with others means that she must go along with their ideas. It might be time for her to consider spending less time with these friends and finding friends with whom she has common interests. You might be able to relieve some of the pressure by suggesting that she could blame "family rules" when she says no to her friends. Sometimes, having a simple excuse like "My parents won't let me" can be a big relief to a child.

Monopolizing the Phone

Our son spends hours talking on the telephone with a friend he sees at school every day. We find it hard to believe there is so much to discuss. The real problem is that no one is able to get through to our home during the evening hours because of the continually busy line.

Many young people make extensive use of the telephone, and these conversations can serve many important purposes. Discussions with friends allow them to share their views. They can respond to each other's ideas and learn to understand themselves and others.

Acceptance by someone outside the family unit is exciting and adds to a child's self-esteem. Defining limits concerning the use of the telephone would be one way to allow your son to enjoy the advantages of telephone time without being inconsiderate of others in the family. An important part of family living is consideration for others. This sounds like the perfect time for your family to work out a telephone schedule.

Children may exclude each other one minute and be best of friends the next. Parents must learn to listen to their children's problems and frustrations without becoming vindictive or emotionally caught up in them. Many of the preceding situations have suggested the potential frustration and pain of friendship. Parental support and confidence are extremely helpful to a child's social growth.

Liking others and being liked is vital for social development. Once a child forms one good friendship it becomes easier to expand the circle of friends. Children who are well liked usually have feelings of self-worth. Those who are disliked often feel inadequate or incompetent. These negative feelings can result in a child's withdrawing or becoming aggressive to gain needed attention. Through trial and error, children gradually come to understand the complexities of friendship. They learn to establish and maintain special relationships that enhance self-esteem.

CONCLUSION

If goals for effective parenting were placed in order of importance, the creation of self-esteem in one's children should probably come first. How children feel about themselves is probably the most important aspect of their lives. It can affect their physical health, their mental abilities, and their interactions with others.

The suggestions throughout this chapter emphasize the importance of helping children to like themselves. When their sense of inner security is nourished, children have the strong foundation necessary for later success.

HELPING CHILDREN DEVELOP THEIR MINDS

Parents can have tremendous influence on the development of their children's minds. Parental influence begins at birth, and it is unending.

Babies benefit from parents who continually talk to them and try to understand their attempts at communication. Children's verbal skills are increased through these exchanges. Their mental development is aided by environmental stimulation and by parental love and support. It is important for children to believe that their own ideas have meaning and are worth communicating.

Parents can damage a child's natural quest for knowledge. One of the easiest ways is to fill home life with anxiety-producing quiz shows. If children constantly believe they must come up with right answers, then the need to please adults will cloud the joy of learning. Parents should encourage the process of figuring things out and, whenever possible, finding more than one answer to the same problem. This exploration needs to be unpressured, to help children realize that learning can and should be fun.

While children need parents who are actively involved in their mental development, they also need time alone for self-discovery. Young children can spend hours creating their own intellectual experiences and challenges. These self-initiated efforts lead to exciting discoveries and encourage mental development.

The following sections consider the impact of family, school, peers, and leisure-time activities on the development of children's minds.

ABILITY TESTING

Unfortunately, many parents and teachers assess a child's intelligence on the basis of test scores. These tests merely offer information on some limited aspects of a child's intellect. Much valuable information about a child's mind cannot be measured through a test. Observation of a child's daily activities, over a prolonged period, enables a more valid assessment of the child's intellectual potential.

Intelligence tests compare children's potentials for academic achievement at particular age levels. Their results point out individual differences in intellectual talents. There seems to be a correlation between high intelligence quotient (IQ) scores and top grades in most public schools. In other words, IQ scores can be used to predict public school success.

Intelligence test results have been used successfully in identifying deficiencies. Sometimes one area of academic weakness can begin to undermine the rest of the school experience. Accurately assessed weaknesses can often be overcome through tutorial help that bolsters a child's skills and self-confidence.

Some problems are worth noting, to help keep IQ tests in proper perspective. First, an accurate IQ score must be derived from several tests, not just one. How a child does on any one test is affected by his or her feelings (both emotional and physical) when taking it. The attitude of the person administering the test may cause children to feel relaxed or anxious. Second, tests are not always culturally fair; they make assumptions about the background of the children taking the test—that they are from middle-class homes, for example—and thus make it difficult for children who do not fit that mold to score well. Finally, IQ scores are not static; they can vary by ten or twenty points within one year's time. The expectations of parents and teachers can affect this variation.

It is important to keep in mind that an IQ test cannot measure specific talents, such as artistic, musical, and physical skills, or human-relations skills, such as social adjustment, emotional maturity, adaptability, dependability, leadership ability, and sense of humor. Nor can it measure motivation, task commitment, attention span, specialized skills and interests, job competency, or curiosity. This incomplete list includes characteristics and talents that can dramatically affect a student's success in school and in life. Children need caring assistance in assessing their strengths and weaknesses. No child should suffer from feelings of inadequacy because of a low IQ score. The following concerns of parents point out some of the potential problems, along with suggestions for handling them.

Ability Grouping   *My nine-year-old son loves to read on his own, and our family enjoys reading together. He has always been in the high reading group at school, but after some testing last month, the teacher moved him to the middle reading group. He is very upset about this. My husband is furious and wants to tell the teacher what a mistake she has made.*

Some teachers do use test scores to determine potential levels of learning among their students. Often the students with high scores receive preferential treatment. It probably isn't coincidental that your son was switched shortly after the testing, but only the teacher can verify this.

Encourage your son to talk with the teacher. He needs to express how he is feeling about the change in reading groups. He could even request another chance to work in the top group. He will grow by constructively working on his own problem. If he tries and feels unhappy about the results, then you might request a parent-teacher conference.

Bright and Isolated   *My twelve-year-old daughter has a very high IQ and seems old for her age. Every adult she talks with tells her how brilliant she is. The problem is that she doesn't even try to get along with her peers. She eats alone at lunchtime, and she refuses to invite anyone home with her after school. She also rejects the kids in our neighborhood. When I try to talk with her about this, she claims the kids are "too stupid."*

Your daughter needs help in learning how to relate to peers so that she will not have to endure a lonely existence. While few children will be her intellectual match, you can help her to discover and appreciate the strengths of each person she meets.

Find some after-school or weekend enrichment classes that will interest and challenge your daughter. During these classes she might begin to communicate with her peers. As children work together to conquer new skills, discussion is inevitable. A book-discussion group might be a way to meet other bright and highly verbal children. Volunteering in a community agency, such as a hospital, nursery school, or convalescent home, would also encourage her to reach out and connect with others.

Our son took IQ tests to help determine where he should be placed in school. He scored very high for his age and grade, so we have had him enrolled in the gifted program in our school system for the last two years. Unfortunately, he has earned average grades and no longer considers himself smart. We are upset about this change and wonder how to handle it.

Gifted or Regular Classes

Intelligence quotients indicate how a child's mental ability compares with the average for the entire population, and IQ tests can be used to predict success in typical public schools. The gifted classes that your son attends are undoubtedly filled with students who have high IQ scores. Consequently, the competition for grades is rigorous. Help your son to understand that he is intelligent but functioning in a competitive academic environment.

There is a lot more to intelligence and to life than receiving good grades. Perhaps he is taking the time to have some fun instead of spending all of his free hours studying. Discuss the importance of being a well-rounded person.

Along with the fun, however, your son should be receiving a sound education and developing good study skills. You could consider having him return to the regular classes where he'll feel more competent and successful.

The teacher just called to tell us our daughter is academically gifted and should be moved into a gifted class. Our daughter loves this teacher and the children in her classroom. We have heard that the kids in the gifted class are

Bright but Obnoxious Classmates

arrogant and obnoxious. We don't want our daughter to pick up that behavior or to lose the friendships she has in her present classroom.

Rest assured that arrogant and obnoxious children can be found in regular classrooms as well as in those for the gifted. Help your daughter to understand that everyone has strengths and weaknesses. Students who show off their intelligence certainly need help with improving their human-relations skills.

Should you decide to move your daughter into the gifted class, help her make plans for maintaining her old friendships as well as forming new ones. Perhaps the school would permit her to join the old class for certain daily activities. Also help her to understand that the move would provide the academic challenge that her mind needs. Children are often able to adapt to new situations with ease.

Rejection because of Test Scores

We just received very depressing news. Our son was rejected by a computer camp that he had his heart set on attending next summer. I called to find out why, and they said they gave him some tests when he was interviewed. They rejected him because he didn't score high enough. What should I tell him?

There is no reason for him to suffer feelings of rejection over this incident. Simply explain that the camp didn't have enough room for everyone who wanted to go there. The camp may be looking for "gifted" children, the small minority who score extremely high on certain intelligence tests. They did not turn your son down because there is anything wrong with him. They probably turned him down because he would have been too pressured if he tried to compete with the children in that camp. There are other computer camps he can attend, ones whose standards are more in keeping with your son's abilities.

Average Isn't Good Enough for Dad

My husband feels our daughter could be doing a lot better in school. She doesn't spend much time on homework, but she manages to pass everything and get a few good grades. She has a lot of friends and hobbies. I'm getting tired of this constant battle about grades between my husband and my daughter.

If your daughter was a continual underachiever, the school probably would have called you. Your husband might want to check out his concerns with the teacher. Perhaps your daughter is an average student who is working to the best of her ability. The fact that she passes everything and has friends and hobbies are all positive signs.

Your husband might try to motivate your daughter to have more interest in academics. He could help her to locate material for a report, they could conduct a science experiment together, or they might build something for a classroom project. It is important that your daughter not feel pressured or inadequate. She should know she has the support of both parents.

My son used to miss going to school when it was vacation time. He was so happy when classes began. Now everything has changed. He was tested in second grade, and the school found that he is gifted. He was moved to a classroom for children with high IQ scores. I am embarrassed to say that during his first three months in this new classroom, he has begun bed-wetting and stuttering. When I wake him up to get ready for school, he says he doesn't feel well and wants to stay home.

Gifted but Too Pressured

You are observing some serious warning signals that things are not right and must change. Your son's nervous reactions have gone far past those expected during an initial adjustment period to the new classroom. Encourage your son to talk with you. Try to find out how he is feeling. He may feel pressured by the accelerated academic pace. Perhaps there is a problem with the teacher or his peers. The more you know about why he is upset, the more helpful your intervention can be. But if he is unable to express his feelings, don't pressure him.

Schedule a conference with your son's teacher at the earliest possible date. Tell the teacher your concerns and ask for ideas to help reduce the stress that your son is feeling. He needs a lot of reassurance at home and at school. The teacher may be quite helpful. If the problem persists, however, you might consider removing your son from this classroom and possibly even seeking professional counseling for him. Your goal should be to help your son regain his positive feelings about school.

High IQ, Weak Reading Skills

Our nine-year-old daughter is in a gifted class. She does really well in math, but reading is more of a struggle for her. Since she is gifted, we can't understand why she doesn't read as well as the others in this classroom.

A small percentage of children are classified as gifted, and an even smaller percentage are gifted in many academic areas. Every classroom, both gifted and regular, includes a wide range of academic ability. It is unfair to expect children who are gifted to be outstanding in everything.

First, make certain that your daughter's vision is not the problem by having her eyes checked. If it proves normal—which, considering her age, is quite likely— help her recognize and appreciate her strengths. Emphasize that she should do the best she can, without comparing her to her classmates. If you think there might be some problem behind her reading struggles, talk with her teacher. There are reading specialists who test children and plan tutorial sessions to solve easily corrected reading problems.

Search for some books that would really capture your daughter's interest and would be relatively easy for her to read. Take turns reading to each other. Do not insist on absolute accuracy—provide help only when she asks for it. Discuss the content and together make guesses about what will happen in the story. This will help her to experience the pleasure of reading.

My son's school has three math groups in each classroom, **Name-calling**
and my son has always been in the lowest group. The other
kids tease the children in this group and call them "dum-
mies." I know my son has a lot of trouble with math, but
I hate to see him in tears over being called names.

You and your son could ask for a meeting with the
teacher. Let the teacher know what is happening and
how your son feels about it. The intent of ability grouping is to help children learn at an appropriate level,
one that will present a challenge. Unfortunately, children sometimes tease each other about these ability
levels. Help your son to identify areas in which he
excels, both in and out of school. When classmates
tease him, encourage him to give a response like "I
know I have a lot of trouble with math, but I'm great
at spelling and volleyball." It is hard to tease someone
who accepts his weaknesses and knows his strengths.
As he reminds his peers of what he does well, he'll
also remind himself.

The concerns in this section have pointed out some of the problems involved with ability grouping and tests. Children with high scores often
receive special attention and face academic pressure. Children with low
scores may be placed in groups that become a butt of peer ridicule. Sadly,
parents and teachers may consider it useless to encourage those children,
assuming incorrectly that their ability is too limited.

An ability test score should be viewed as merely one of many pieces
of information about a child. Far more is needed to give a full picture of
a child's intellectual potential. Many important aspects of a child's mind
cannot be tested. Furthermore, IQ scores are not fixed for life. They can
increase or decrease in response to environmental influences. To give each
child a fair chance for growth, schools and parents must consider more
than test scores. Observation of children in daily activities is essential to
an accurate assessment of mental ability.

OTHER SCHOOL-RELATED ISSUES

Parents have tremendous influence on their children's attitudes about school
and about teachers. Children carefully observe their parents' reactions to
their stories about what goes on at school and listen with great interest to
what their parents say after a visit to school. If parents display a positive

attitude toward the school, their children are more likely to be successful and happy there.

A more subtle but powerful influence on children's learning is their parents' own interest in education. If parents ask questions, take classes, read, or simply appear interested in acquiring knowledge, children will believe that learning is an important part of life. The following concerns and suggestions point out a number of ways for parents to be constructively involved in their children's schooling.

Dislike of Teacher

Day after day my daughter complains about her third-grade teacher. I happen to know that this teacher has had a wonderful reputation for many years. That makes it hard to respond to my daughter's continual complaints.

Let your daughter know that you want to hear her complaints and feelings about this teacher. If she knows that you value her opinions, she will continue to share them with you. If she thinks that you are going to ignore her thoughts, she'll eventually stop sharing them. Children must feel free to express their opinions at home.

Help your daughter figure out whether she has specific reasons for disliking her teacher or whether her dislike is just a vague, general feeling. It is possible that they are having a personality conflict. If there are solvable problems, you can be helpful. Suggest alternative solutions to your daughter and let her pick one that might work. There probably isn't a teacher in existence who is liked by every student. Your daughter could have an excellent growth experience this year if she learns how to successfully survive having a teacher that she doesn't like.

Tell your daughter the good things you have heard about the teacher and ask if she finds any of them to be true. One morning before school, tell your daughter that you have a special assignment for her. Ask her to watch the teacher carefully that day and find one good thing about her. The assignment might lessen her dislike of her teacher.

From time to time, find reasons to drop nice notes

to the teacher. These notes might concern an interesting assignment she gave or anything else you can, with sincerity, write a kind note about. Teachers generally receive too few of these notes from parents. Positive contacts between you and the teacher will set an example that could ultimately help your daughter overcome her negative attitude toward the teacher.

I moved to a new neighborhood so that my son would be **Reading Readiness**
able to attend a certain school; a lot of people told me it is the best place in town for bright children and I know my son is smart as a whip. But he still doesn't know how to read even though he is finishing first grade. I just found out that the school has a policy of not teaching children to read until they are in second grade. Until then, students spend a lot of time on what is called "reading readiness." Their "projects" include turning the classroom into a store or into another country. I can't figure out what sense this makes.

Perhaps you should make an appointment to talk with your son's teacher, and possibly the principal. They will be able to help you understand the philosophy behind their reading program.

Many educators believe that few children would have reading problems if schools waited until second grade to teach reading. Reading skills are dependent on physical growth and development. By age seven, most children have reached a maximum point of development for learning to read, which permits easier and more effective learning. Of course, many children can learn to read much earlier, but premature exposure is not always an advantage. True reading readiness occurs when children are physically, mentally, and emotionally ready. Then the process is smooth and satisfying.

You mentioned that your son's classroom is sometimes "turned into" a store or another country. These are exactly the kinds of projects that spark children's interest. Many academic skills can be learned while children are having fun. These activities can provide opportunities to increase vocabularies, solve problems, and develop a variety of other skills that are foundations for reading.

Reflective Learners

My daughter has heard the same complaint from her teachers all the way through school. Her fourth-grade teacher just told her that she's far too bright to take so long to grasp things. It seems she asks a number of questions about assignments and the teacher loses patience. Today she told my daughter to just plunge into the work and forget all of her questions. This questioning seems natural for my daughter, but her teachers certainly think it is wrong.

Some children are reflective learners—that is, they need to move slowly with new material. The fact that they take their time and ask questions does not mean that they are learning less than their faster-paced classmates. In fact, they frequently make fewer errors, as they feel very sure of themselves before moving forward.

There is a danger in your daughter's hearing this complaint over and over again. She could come to view herself as slow or not bright enough, and that could discourage her from trying at all.

There are several things you might do to help her. First of all, point out that her academic record speaks for itself. She has done very well, and the teachers call her "bright." This means she has been a success in school. Second, help your daughter learn how to listen to directions. Hold practice sessions in which you give her instructions of various kinds and teach her how to take accurate notes as the instructions are given. Once she learns to write down her assignments, she can go over her notes many times without bothering the teacher. Third, suggest she find several classmates who might discuss the assignments with her at school or on the phone at home. Last, and most important of all, help her to understand that there is *nothing* wrong with her!

We have two children attending the same elementary school. **Homework**
*Our younger one has homework every day and demands
our help constantly. My wife is worried that our older one
won't get enough out of this academic year because his
teacher doesn't believe in homework. We have gone to their
school conferences, and both children seem to be doing
fine.*

Some children improve their level of achievement
through homework, but many do not. Each teacher
has the right to set a homework policy. This year your
children's teachers obviously have very differing views.
As long as your child is doing well in school, go along
with the teacher's policy. If the child is asking for
homework, then perhaps you or your wife could create
a few challenging assignments.

Insist that your younger child stop demanding
your help. After all, the assignment is given to the
student, not the parent. Parents can help their children
by providing them with well-lit, orderly, and quiet
places to work. Children might also need help in using
the dictionary and locating reference material, or in
setting up a logical plan of action to complete a difficult
assignment. When children need to study for tests, it
can be helpful for a parent to quiz them. However,
the quizzing is detrimental to the child if the parent
becomes upset or punitive. Children need support
rather than pressure. A calm, caring parent can offer
minimal assistance with homework and still be really
encouraging.

Our son is in second grade, and he is very bright. He likes **Sloppy Handwriting**
*going to school and thinks his teacher is wonderful, but
my husband considers the teacher "incompetent." Our son
frequently brings home sloppy-looking papers that the
teacher has marked "good" or "excellent." My husband
feels that the teacher should demand better work and put
more critical comments on the papers.*

Bright six- and seven-year-old boys often demonstrate

fine thinking but sloppy handwriting. Their eye-hand coordination is not as well developed as that of girls their age; it may be difficult for them to sit calmly and write neatly. Your son's teacher seems to value the content of his thoughts, and the comments encourage him. The teacher is probably aware of how typical sloppy handwriting is for boys of this age.

Your son is at the beginning of his academic career. Your husband should support his efforts and refrain from undermining the teacher. If your husband continues to make negative comments about your son's work and about his teacher, it could harm your child's attitude toward school. Perhaps your husband could be encouraged to have a constructive conversation directly with your son's teacher.

Grades

Whenever I ask my daughter how things are going at school, she tells me what she thinks she'll get on her next report card. There is so much more to school than grades. It makes me sad to see the academic emphasis placed on grades rather than on the day-to-day process of learning.

Your daughter is lucky that you have such an enlightened attitude about the purpose of school. Many students consider themselves failures when they don't achieve high grades. Some work only to please parents and teachers or to avoid their disapproval. In these situations, the motivation to learn can be ruined by anxiety over poor grades. An obsession with grades can be harmful. The related anxiety can make learning so unpleasant that some children just give up.

Teachers and parents can help students evaluate their own academic performance. Identifying areas for improvement and areas of strength can help children assess themselves realistically. It is important for each student to try to do his or her best work. The level of achievement is less important than the fact that there is genuine effort.

Rephrase your questions about school to help your daughter shift her attention away from grades. You might ask her what is the most interesting thing that she learned that day, or the best question that she asked. Create a list of questions to ask her so that you won't fall into the habit of asking the same thing every day. Your sincere interest in your daughter's education encourages the learning process.

I have noticed that our children seem anxious when we **Conferences**
go to their parent-teacher conferences. My husband and I always tell them to relax, because they are good kids and really don't have anything to worry about. Our words don't seem to help.

We can better understand how children feel about conferences when we imagine important people in our lives meeting to discuss us. We might easily feel just as anxious. Requesting the teacher's permission to bring your child to the conference could diminish a lot of the concern. Some parents and teachers have been pleasantly surprised by children's contributions to conferences. Other children prefer to listen quietly. Either way, the child can hear exactly what is being discussed rather than imagine the worst. If it is not possible for children to attend the conferences, take notes on the important points discussed and any decisions that were made. Then go over your notes with your children; this will help avoid misunderstandings and allow the children to be included in the conference process. However you go about it, the important thing is to build trust between parents, teachers, and students. This relationship is an important foundation for children's success in school.

Bright children who learn easily often excel in school. They can experience success with little effort. However, if they are not challenged academically, they can become bored and restless. Children who find school too difficult will also become restless and so discouraged that the effort involved in learning doesn't seem worthwhile. Academic achievers, underachievers, and average students all need their parents' support. When children go to school they leave the security of home and enter a world where the approval of teachers and peers must be earned. Parents need to convince their children that they can and will meet both the academic and the interpersonal challenges of school. Continual open communication with children and occasional contacts with the school will keep parents in close touch with their children's school experiences.

Teachers have so many students that it is difficult for them to monitor the feelings and moods of each child. Sometimes teachers do not recognize problems before they become explosive. If parents stay in touch with their children's attitudes about school, they can work on problems at home and alert the teacher if necessary. It is important to recognize problems early, before they become more serious. Parents need to consider themselves partners with the schools.

DEVELOPING CREATIVITY

All newborns have creative potential, which increases when nurtured and can diminish when neglected. We can observe creativity even in children who are very young, by the way they talk, move, and play. Children derive satisfaction from the process of being creative. Parents who encourage their babies' explorations are enabling creativity to develop. Constant restrictions are detrimental to this process.

Play offers children opportunities to do things in new and different ways, to display imagination and spontaneity—in other words, to be creative. Creative play helps children learn about themselves and their world: what they can and cannot do, what they like and dislike, what is difficult and what is easy.

Certain characteristics seem to be consistently present among children whose creativity is encouraged. These children raise questions, view issues from different sides, and suggest original, unconventional solutions to problems. They are often open to new ideas and suggestions, which indicates flexibility. Their ideas are fresh and often whimsical. The following examples include numerous suggestions of ways for parents to encourage creativity.

Creativity and IQ   *The counselor at our son's school just said that we should plan a vocational program for our son's high school years. He pointed out that our son scored near the bottom of his class on the IQ test and that he doesn't do well with academics. The counselor feels that because our son will never make it into college it is wrong to set him up for a disappointment. For years our son has been creating floor plans for houses and buildings. He says that some day he wants to be an architect. He uses a ruler and draws these* *buildings to scale. If he is so dumb, how can he do all of this?*

Intelligence tests are limited in what they can measure. They do not, for example, measure spatial perception or artistic ability. Do not give your son the impression that he should give up trying because he hasn't done well in school so far. Try to find classes where he will be able to use his special talents. You might also consider some tutoring to bolster his academic skills.

Some creative children are bored with traditional academic routines. Your son might surprise you and improve his academic record in junior high and high school. The added variety he will encounter there may provide the challenge he needs. Your son's desire to be an architect could give him the necessary motivation to succeed.

Create or Conform?

My daughter seems to do everything in her unique way. She uses toys in ways that I'm sure the manufacturer never imagined. Her drawings always attract attention because nothing about them is typical. Her use of color, shape, and size is amazing. We have always appreciated this quality, but her teachers do not like her maverick ways. We cannot afford a private school, so she needs to learn how to survive in public school. How can we make it easier for her?

Continue to let your daughter know that you appreciate the many forms that her creativity takes. Also help her to understand that many people, including even some teachers, do not appreciate things that are different. Your daughter needs to know when she must follow the rules and when it is all right to be original. Eventually, she may have a teacher who appreciates her creativity; meanwhile, she should conform in school and you should provide ample out-of-school opportunities for her to exercise her talents. Have art supplies handy and seek out community programs that will channel her creative energies. Parks, recreation centers, and clubs for children often have such programs, usually at little or no cost.

"Inventions"

Often when I come home from work, I find my six-year-old son has made a number of "inventions" with my tools. I don't really like my tools being used. My wife says I should leave our son alone because he is being creative. I wonder if she's just indulging him or if there really is something to this?

Your wife is wise to recognize the importance of your son's concoctions. He is at an age where being inventive is important to his development. This is also a time when he could become embarrassed over negative reactions to his work.

Put away the tools that would be dangerous for him to use, but let him use the others. Show him how to use them safely and how to care for them, and explain that he must return them when done. You could encourage his creations by buying him some tools and supplies of his own. You might be the parents of a future famous inventor!

Peer Influence on Creativity

As an artist, I value creativity in my children. I am upset that my daughter insists on playing only popular tunes on the piano and refuses to create the kind of original music that she used to play. Her drawings consist of rainbows and butterflies, because that's what her fifth-grade girl-friends draw. I can't seem to convince her to explore her unique talents.

Your daughter's behavior is typical for her age, when children often want to conform to their peer culture. Stop trying to convince her to create as she used to. Accept and appreciate the way she is at this point in her life. From time to time, mention her original tunes of the past and ask her to play one for you. Enjoy looking at her old paintings. Her creativity will not disappear and could return sooner if she doesn't feel pressured.

Messy Art Projects

My sister and I totally disagree on where children should

experience art. She takes her children to classes at an art studio where they have professional guidance. She feels I'm encouraging my children to mess up the house because art projects are allowed in the kitchen. I feel their projects are worth the trouble of cleaning up afterwards, and I don't think that young children need professional art teachers.

You and your sister are using different approaches to provide artistic experiences for your children. If your sister is upset by "art messes" in the kitchen, it is far better for her children to do their art projects at a studio. At home or at the studio, children should help clean up after they have had the fun of making a mess. If the atmosphere is relaxed and the emphasis is on the pleasure of the experience, working with art materials can be an enriching part of growing up.

Our daughter spends hours creating wonderful dances. We decided to enroll her in dance classes with a very respected modern dance teacher. This teacher asked all of the parents simply to encourage our children to dance at home and to refrain from telling them what we like about their dances or which ones we like the best. We're not sure this makes much sense.

Performing for Approval

You are paying a respected professional to teach your daughter dancing. While there are not hard-and-fast rules about "right" and "wrong" ways to encourage children, your child's teacher has expressed a specific preference. Whenever you question a suggestion like this, don't hesitate to ask the teacher for reasons; it might make more sense when the explanation is understood. It could be that the teacher does not want her students dancing to please their parents. When children dance for the purpose of pleasing others, they can easily forget to enjoy the process.

I think my son has artistic talent. The sad thing is that we live in a small apartment, so we have neither indoor space

Lack of Space

nor a yard for creative projects. I don't have the money to enroll him in special classes. I had hoped his school would provide art opportunities, but when I went to open house I noticed that every child's picture looked the same. I asked the teacher about this, and she proudly explained that the children have really learned how to copy the drawings she shows them. I don't know what to do.

In the future your son may have other teachers who value individuality over copying. In the meantime, a small apartment does have plenty of space for creative play: The refrigerator or bathtub can provide a temporary "canvas" for washable paints; a fort made of blankets over a table offers a perfect hideaway; a cookie sheet by the kitchen sink is a good surface for finger painting with shaving cream; a box of toothpicks, a roll of string, and a flat piece of Styrofoam or cork can provide hours of inexpensive fun for a creative child. Your son is fortunate that you want to provide creative opportunities for him. Your apartment is limited only if you do not take time to think of suitable activities.

Tired Parent

Before I became a parent, I had dreams of helping my children become creative contributors to society. As a parent, however, the reality of daily living leaves me exhausted. After a day of chores, I am hardly in the mood to encourage my son's creativity.

Considerable effort is expended by most people just getting through the day successfully. Parenting demands tremendous effort and increased responsibilities. Unfortunately many parents think that major projects, outings, or large sums of money are necessary to encourage creativity in their children. The necessary daily routine of family living provides many opportunities for fostering creativity. For example, all of you might try eating dinner or brushing your teeth with your nondominant hand. Bathing by candlelight and having a picnic meal on the living room floor are examples of changes in boring routines. Encourage your son to think of some ideas for you.

You will be amazed over the way these cost-free changes prompt conversation and spark enthusiasm. They will also contribute to your goal of fostering creativity in your son.

For as long as I can remember, whenever our son hears music he begins to dance. Even music that is piped into elevators can inspire him. We have always encouraged and praised his love of dance. Recently, some of his schoolmates have begun to tease him and call him a "sissy" because he's always dancing. Our son was embarrassed and upset, but so far we haven't figured out a way to help him deal with this problem.

Teased about Dancing

Peer influence plays a powerful role in the lives of children. It is undoubtedly confusing for your son to be teased about something that is so important in his life. Empathize with the pain he is experiencing without becoming overly involved. Your energy should be used to encourage him to pursue his interest in dancing.

Find out where your son might take dance lessons in your community. Also, make it a habit to check the papers for news about dance performances; when a noted male dancer is to appear on television or in your town, make it a point to watch the show or attend the performance with your son. You might consider inviting some of his friends to join you. Observing the expertise of an outstanding male dancer could inspire your son and encourage his love of dance.

My wife and I both work, so our time with our seven- and nine-year-old daughters is somewhat limited. We finally have a one-month vacation and plan to drive across the country. I think it would be a good idea to spend the time in the car getting to know the children better, and maybe having some good discussions. I need some help in how to work on these goals.

Traveling

There are a number of ways you can plan for a meaningful trip. Ask your friends and co-workers about games they have played with their children during long car rides. Have your children gather ideas from their friends. Together you can then create a list of possible activities. Billboards, road signs, and license plates offer material for alphabet and number games. Listing types of cars, animals, colors, and so on can be fun to do and, at the same time, stimulate awareness.

The time spent together in the car offers opportunities to discuss feelings and thoughts that we often neglect in our busy daily routines. You could prepare a list of questions that would provide a starting point. To get you started, here are some sample questions:

Questions about the Past:
What is one of your first memories?
List some of the funniest, scariest, and saddest things that have ever happened to you.
If you could relive one event in your life, which one would it be and why?
Do you remember what your favorite activities were when you were little?

Questions about the Present:
If you could have anything you wanted for dinner, what would you choose?
Who is your favorite person outside of the immediate family and why?
What is one thing you would like to change about your life?
If you had a million dollars, what would you do with it?
What are two of the things you like best about each person in this car?
Describe your idea of a perfect day.

Questions about the Future:
Twenty years from now what would you like to be doing in your everyday life?
How do you want to spend vacation time in the future?
If it were in your power to change the world, in what ways would you change it?

If you could take six people with you to explore a newly discovered island, who would you take and why?

As you take the time to get to know your children in new ways during this trip, they will also be getting to know their parents in new and different ways. The trip will undoubtedly be a positive experience for all of you.

These concerns and suggestions demonstrated some of the ways in which parents can encourage creative behavior in their children. One basic rule for getting along with children is to be flexible and remain aware that there are a variety of ways to deal with any one problem. In daily living, problems arise continually, and there is no one "right way" to deal with them. Parents who continually insist on a "right way" decrease options for creative thought. Showing respect for children's thoughts, actions, and creations demonstrates confidence in their efforts and abilities and encourages creative self-expression.

LEISURE-TIME ACTIVITIES

Even during the school year leisure-time activities generally occupy more hours in a child's day than school. Consequently, parents need to understand the potential impact of these hours. Children's creative development should not be left solely to the schools, as out-of-school activities can have great influence.

In an attempt to stimulate their children's minds, some parents provide too many after-school activities. Too much stimulation can overwhelm a child, who might ultimately resist or withdraw to avoid the bombardment. At the opposite extreme, some children must find their own after-school, weekend, and vacation activities; all too often, their solution is to spend hours passively watching television. While some shows are truly enriching, children need a lot more from their leisure-time activities than they can get by turning a TV dial.

Working out a healthy balance between low-key and stimulating leisure activities is an important part of effective parenting. Children's interests and potential talents should be considered as parents survey the programs available. The following pages point out some of the trials and tribulations parents might face as they help plan their children's leisure time.

I can't get my eight-year-old daughter to understand why   **Forced Practicing**

I make her practice the piano for an hour every day. We fight about it constantly, and she usually ends up in tears. I've decided that it doesn't matter if she cries or doesn't understand my reasoning. I know how much enjoyment piano playing will give her as an adult. Don't you think that someday she'll thank me for forcing her to practice now?

There is no guarantee that your daughter will someday thank you. Many adults still resent being forced to practice piano when they were young. Some have intentionally blocked out everything they learned.

Step back and try to assess the situation. Are you or your daughter deriving any benefits from the piano? Is it worth the daily battle? Is one hour of practice each day too much for an eight-year-old? Are there more positive ways to encourage her practicing? Is the power struggle over the piano adversely affecting your relationship with your daughter? In the long run, a good relationship with one's parents is more important than piano skills.

Perhaps your daughter would prefer another form of artistic expression. If she is inwardly motivated, then putting forth the effort required won't cause such a struggle.

Brothers Competing

We have two sons who are very close in age—one nine and a half, the other eleven. We have always given them the same opportunities to participate in out-of-school programs. These include not only sports, but also programs in science, art, photography, and a number of other subjects. The younger boy somehow excels in everything he tries, while the older one struggles along and really has to work to keep up with his brother. We feel sorry for him because he can't help resenting his younger brother. We don't know how to handle this.

Your younger son is fortunate to excel in so many ways. Your older son should be complimented for his perseverance; the willingness to strive is an admirable quality and should not be overlooked.

Help each son select the activities that he likes best. Then let the two of them attend different programs. This will undoubtedly mean some extra driving for you, but eventually it will be worth the effort. Your older son will have a chance at succeeding without comparing himself unfavorably with his brother. This can only enhance family life for all of you.

My daughter loves the water and begged us for swimming lessons. She enjoys every minute of her lessons and wants to practice her strokes whenever possible. I have visited her class a few times, and it is obvious that the other children have more style and swimming talent than my daughter. She insists that eventually she'll make the local swim team, and she wants to be an Olympic swimming champion. Do you think I should let her put so much of herself into swimming when she really doesn't have a chance at succeeding?

Lack of Talent

So much of what it takes to be a star in any field is interest, determination, perseverance, and practice. Although natural talent is important, it is not enough. It is a mistake to prejudge children; they often surprise us and themselves. Let your daughter continue with her dream. She isn't doing anything harmful. In a few years she might decide to change to a sport in which she displays more talent. She may even surprise you and become an Olympic champion someday!

The teachers at school say my son has musical talent and should learn to play an instrument. I have encouraged him, but he has gone from violin to guitar to drums, all within one year. I have spent a lot of money on equipment and lessons. While I want him to explore his musical talent, I do not have unlimited finances.

Rapidly Shifting Interests

Children need to find out which instruments they like before they can make a serious commitment. Try to locate instruments you can borrow or rent for a while;

this will be a lot less expensive than buying them. Perhaps your son could help cover the costs by working around the house.

Generally, one must master a musical instrument to a certain point in order to derive satisfaction from it. If your son begins and then drops a new musical challenge too rapidly, he will not accomplish enough to know any enjoyment. Before you invest any additional money, insist that he make a reasonable time commitment to a new instrument. Then help him stick with it. An important life lesson is learning that we do have the capacity to tolerate frustration. Assure your son that pleasure will follow the initial hard work. After he has fulfilled the initial commitment, let your son decide whether he is going to stop or continue.

Boredom

Unless I plan activities for the weekend, I end up having to listen to my daughter whine and say "I'm bored." Don't you think a ten-year-old should make plans for herself? I resent using the entire weekend to entertain her; I need relaxation for myself, to prepare for another workweek.

Your daughter has undoubtedly come to expect you to plan interesting weekends because you have consistently taken this responsibility. Have a friendly talk with her about how you feel, and work together to set up a plan for the weekends. At the beginning, perhaps you could plan one weekend day and have her plan the next. Help her make up a list of friends and relatives she could call and activities she might plan with them. Along with the "people-centered" list, she also needs a list of enjoyable things to do on her own. Children need to develop resources to meet their own needs. The lists should have both stimulating and calm activities. The next time your daughter feels bored, have her get out her lists and use them to plan activities.

Stamp Collecting

My son has been collecting stamps for several years. He

spends hours arranging them in scrapbooks. He's not particularly interested in sharing his hobby with anyone, and somehow it doesn't seem to be going anywhere. Should I try to encourage him to build models or take up some other kind of hobby that has a finished product?

Hobbies are frequently centered around an interest that is self-generated. Because the hobby is voluntarily chosen, it tends to sustain itself over time. Many hobbyists derive satisfaction from the effort they expend rather than from a finished product.

The open-ended hobby of stamp collecting obviously has absorbed your son. He is choosing to spend hours working with his scrapbooks because he likes the process. He may be learning far more than you realize from this hobby. Stamp collecting involves the skills of classification and organization. Your son might also become interested in world geography as he tracks the origins of his stamps. You should intervene only if he wants to work with his collection during all of his leisure hours. He needs time for activities with friends.

My husband loves to relax in front of the television set. He prefers the shows with a lot of action and violence. Yesterday, after a particularly violent show, our daughter punched her girlfriend really hard. Both of our children beg for every item they see advertised on television. They like to keep the set on even when they are playing with their toys. I can't stand to hear it any more, and I'd like to get rid of it. I think it would help us get rid of a lot of family problems. **Television**

Getting rid of the television set is one solution, but it sounds as if you would be outvoted by your family. You have raised a number of important issues related to children and television. First of all, research studies do indicate that television violence can encourage aggressive, physical behavior in children. On TV programs, violence is portrayed as acceptable behavior.

By watching this casual violence, children become less sensitive to violence in general. Second, children see hundreds of television commercials each week. Few parents could or should buy all the products that commercials teach children to want. Third, if the set is on all the time, television watching can easily become a habit that is hard to break. Children need a lot of leisure-time hours to explore other activities.

Parents need to limit the amount of time children spend watching television, to avoid having them spend too many passive hours. They also need to monitor the quality of the shows. A number of programs are filled with useful information and provide excellent opportunities for children, but others prompt undesirable thoughts and feelings in children. Children differ from each other in their reactions to the same show, depending on their particular sensitivities or reactions to violence, humor, suspense, and sorrow. Be alert to shows that seem to prompt negative responses in your children, such as excessive anxiety, sleeplessness, bad dreams, increased fears, or aggressive behavior. Tell them how you see the shows affecting them so that they will understand why you are restricting their viewing.

Your active participation in your children's television viewing can make it an enriching experience for them. Help them to be critical and evaluate the programs that they do see. This will increase their thinking skills and help them to be less gullible. Ask how they would feel if they were treated the way some of the characters are treated. Tell them when you find something on a TV show unbelievable and seek their opinions. Many serious problems are presented, explored, and resolved within the brief time block of a typical show. Discuss how rarely this would happen in real life. When your children ask for products seen on television, buy several and let them compare the differences between what the advertisements promise and what the actual products deliver. With your guidance, your children can become informed consumers. They also will become selective about which TV shows to watch.

My husband wants our children, ages eight and ten, to go away to camp this summer. He feels it will be an enriching experience for them. I'm not sure it is worth spending the money because I think they will get homesick.

Summer Camp

Even if children feel homesick, there can be a lot of benefits to attending camp. They have the opportunity to learn how to get along without their parents. Many children experience tremendous social and emotional growth as a result of successful camp experiences.

It is important that you select a camp carefully, as carefully as you would select a day-care center or a community with good schools. Sensitive counselors know how to help homesick children. Fine camping programs keep children busy with a wide variety of activities so that they don't have time to dwell on homesickness. You might also want to talk with your children about what to do if they do feel homesick; they could write you, talk with a counselor, or share their feelings with each other. They should go to camp anticipating a good time rather than worrying about missing you.

Many of our son's classmates play team sports after school and on the weekends. Unfortunately, our son prefers ice skating and roller-skating on his own. We want him to experience being a team member, but he refuses. We don't know whether we should make him join a team or just forget it.

Team vs. Individual Sports

Encourage your son to pursue the sports he enjoys. Perhaps at the rink he can find other skaters he would enjoy as friends. Talk with the rink instructors about the possibility of a group performance so the skaters could experience the necessary cooperative efforts of such an undertaking. Some children avoid team sports because they don't like the group pressure to perform and win. Sometimes teammates, parents, and coaches get carried away with winning, and make that their sole focus. The screaming and yelling is too much for some children. A competitive team experience can certainly be beneficial, but it shouldn't be mandatory for all children.

Video Games and Computers

Our sons never used to be sociable, but during the last six months that has changed. One is obsessed with video games and spends all the time he can playing them. The other is so engrossed in computers that he rarely talks about anything else. The phone rings constantly with calls from the new friends who share their interests. Now we long for the good old quiet days, and we worry that our boys have one-track minds.

A healthy variety is a plus in anyone's daily schedule, but some activities, including those your boys have selected, tend to consume all of the participants' free time, at least in the early stages when there is much to learn and many new challenges. If you approve of the new friends they are making, then be glad that a whole new world has opened up to them.

There are many similarities between your boys' current pursuits. Each activity has its own unique vocabulary and skills, each requires logical thinking and concentration, and each seems to sustain interest over long periods. Your children will feel a strong sense of accomplishment as they master these activities.

It is important for each of your boys to share interests with peers. Their leisure-time pursuits have led to both new friendships and new skills. The benefits seem well worth the changes your family is facing.

Children need many opportunities to explore their interests. During the exploratory phase, some will discover special talents. Children who achieve success often will create in themselves expectations and desires to reach greater heights. Self-motivation is the key to developing talents or interests.

Some children participate in an activity for the wrong reasons: they fear parental disapproval if they stop, or they continue only to receive approval. It is preferable for a child to participate because the activity itself is satisfying. Children should not continue with activities for long periods of time just to measure up to their parent's expectations. Some exceptionally talented youngsters lose interest after being pushed too hard, too fast, and for too long. Talent needs to be fostered, not forced. Children generally take on any new challenge with enthusiasm. When this enthusiasm is not matched by a sense of accomplishment and competence, the interest will wane. Losing interest in this way is quite different from giving up at the beginning because it takes work to derive any satisfaction. It is important for parents to show that they value the child's efforts, regardless of the outcome. All children deserve the opportunity to explore some activities free of report cards and adult pressures. Regardless of talent levels, all children can be helped to develop their creativity and have fun with leisure-time activities.

CONCLUSION

The beginning of this chapter discussed the importance of parents' involvement with their children's intellectual development outside school. The section on school-related issues encouraged parents to take an active role in their children's formal education. It is important for parents to show up at school and to know the teachers. If parents consider the school an important place, then children will also. With little effort or time, parents can be school supporters. Administrators and teachers are generally receptive to parents who express their appreciation of the good things that occur at school and who speak up when concerned. Parents must consider themselves partners with the schools in the task of educating their children.

Academic life and peer relationships can prompt children to conform, and this conformity can diminish creativity. When teachers rely heavily on workbook and textbook assignments, children easily become bored. Fortunately, some teachers do encourage creativity. In such classrooms, students are given positive recognition for their contributions.

When children are offered too few opportunities for creative expression in school, parents need to compensate. There is a great deal of leisure time in most children's daily schedules. Some of the leisure hours can be used for structured or unstructured creative explorations. Projects at home and stimulating extracurricular experiences give children many opportunities for creativity. Being introduced to a variety of experiences can spark creative energy in children.

Parents have abundant time to influence their children's intellectual development. That sphere must not remain solely the school's responsibility. Children who feel loved and respected at home have a tremendous advantage. Also fortunate are those children who can experience the excitement of learning and creativity on their own. Perhaps more than any structured activity, unpressured experimentation challenges children to think creatively.

CHAPTER **4**

SELF-ESTEEM

A child's self-esteem reflects many factors, including appearance, mental capacity, relationships with others, and the ability to effect change. The degree to which a child has self-esteem largely determines how he or she reacts to the world. The people who are important to a child—parents, relatives, teachers, friends—can have great impact on that child's self-esteem.

No one acquires self-esteem on a particular day, or at a particular point during maturation; it develops in a continual process and is shaped by each new situation. In general, children fortunate enough to have a good sense of self-esteem respect themselves, feel competent, and feel that they belong, they matter, and they can successfully influence others. These children can tolerate frustration, take risks, and stick with tasks until they are finished, achieving a sense of pride through their accomplishments.

Children with low self-esteem perceive themselves as incapable, insignificant, unsuccessful, and unworthy. They are quick to say negative things about themselves and have a general sense of helplessness about improving their circumstances. They avoid taking risks and getting into situations that could provoke anxiety.

Most children experience both positive and negative feelings about themselves. The goal for parents is to encourage the positive feelings. The following examples show how parents can have a significant impact on their children's evolving self-esteem.

118

The friendliest member of our family is our seven-year-old daughter. She is the first to notice if someone is upset or not feeling well. At home she chatters from morning until night. But at school and other places outside the house she rarely says a word. She has heard countless people refer to her as "shy." We are worried that she might start to believe it.

Shifting Self-Perceptions

At home your daughter undoubtedly feels secure, loved, and capable, so she feels comfortable sharing her thoughts with the entire family. She is still young and probably unsure about the world outside the home, which makes her cautious and withdrawn. In time she will learn to trust herself in the world and to be more open with others.

You can help by inviting family friends over and encouraging her to invite classmates. Learning to enjoy these people in the security of her home will make it easier for her to talk with them elsewhere. All of us feel more secure in comfortable places.

Recently, the first-grade teacher mentioned that my son often seems very sad. Now when we sit down to eat, I can hardly look at my son. The teacher is right; he does look sad. I was very unhappy throughout my childhood and later learned that my father also had an unhappy childhood. Could sadness be inherited?

"Inherited" Sadness

A person's self-concept is acquired, not inherited. A child's self-concept is affected by many factors, the most important being how the child's parents view themselves. Because parents are the most significant role models, children often imitate them.

Perhaps sad moods have come to seem normal to you, and consequently you haven't noticed your son's sadness. Fortunately, his teacher pointed it out and you can be objective enough to recognize the truth. It may be hard for you to look at your son, because you want him to be happy but instead he seems as sad as you were during your own childhood. You know how damaging this pattern can be to a child's developing self-concept.

You might consider seeking professional help* so that your own self-concept can be improved. You will then be able to help your son. He is still young, and both of you can still learn how to derive joy from daily living. If you are determined to find ways to be happier, your son will benefit, and so will you.

Differences between Twins

If anyone had tried to tell me how dramatically different twins could be, I wouldn't have believed them. Some of my sons' classmates were fooling around in school the other day, so the teacher yelled at the whole class. One of my twins shrugged his shoulders and ran out to play. The other cried for a long time and felt awful about the teacher's being so angry. I don't know why he takes things personally and is shattered, while his brother just goes on his merry way.

Even though your boys are twins, they have different ways of thinking and perceiving. As with all children, their reactions to a situation depend on their interpretations of it. Their self-perceptions may differ as dramatically as their reactions. Your less sensitive twin is probably capable of experiencing unpleasant situations without feeling personally responsible or damaged; his sturdy self-image is not ruffled by outbursts like the one at school. In contrast, his brother identifies with each situation, even when he is not directly involved, and ends up feeling guilty.

Your sensitive son's extreme reactions might reflect a shaky self-image. Keep in mind, however, that some sensitive children have grown up to make magnificent contributions to society. Your goal should not be to eradicate his sensitivity but to reduce his insecurities and his tendency to overreact. Encourage family conversations as a part of this process. Ask the twins questions about how they felt in certain situations, such as when the teacher was yelling. Find out why one considered himself guilty and the other knew

*See Appendix I for information on finding help.

he wasn't to blame. Just hearing his brother's reasoning might help the sensitive twin to react with less intensity. Suggest that for one day each pretend to be the other and react to situations the way his brother would. The sensitive twin might find his brother's approach a lot easier and less draining than his own. Any way that you can bolster his self-confidence will undoubtedly help him.

Needing Time Alone

We live in a small apartment with our three children. They have always shared one bedroom and gotten along well. I could always depend on my oldest daughter to look after the younger ones, but recently she's been begging us to give her some time alone in the bedroom. I don't understand this change, so I asked her why. She just says that she wants to be her own person some of the time. I don't want to keep my other children out of their own room. How should I handle this?

Having private time is important to many children, especially as they become adolescents. When this need is respected and observed, children gain a strong sense of individuality. Call a meeting of the whole family and work out a plan that would permit your daughter to have privacy. Arrange for her to have the bedroom to herself for a brief period of time on a regular basis. This will demonstrate respect for her right to privacy and also enable her to experience a sense of control over her personal environment. At the family meeting, explain to the younger ones that when they reach their sister's age they, too, will want time to themselves and will be given that privilege. It may take a while for this new plan to run smoothly, so give it time to work.

Athletic Inadequacy

Naturally, we are pleased when our son feels good about himself. He seems to have pride in his academic accomplishments, his hobbies, his family, and his friends. Even his awkwardness at sports didn't seem to bother him—until now. Most of the boys in his fifth-grade class have joined an after-school soccer team, and that is all they talk about. Suddenly our self-assured son is anxious and upset. He knows he isn't good enough to make the team, and he feels left out. My wife thinks we should get him into some other activities but I'm not sure what is right.

Even children who grow up in ideal early environments and display healthy self-confidence are vulnerable to being hurt. It is impossible to shield a child from all feelings of inadequacy. To a large extent, others determine how we view ourselves. Every person we encounter can confirm or alter our self-concept by his or her attitude toward us.

To attack this problem, you must first look toward the cause. Is your son's awkwardness at sports the result of some sort of physical handicap? If not, has he always been awkward, or is he just going through a phase of rapid growth? And is he really as awkward as you think? You might discuss these matters with his gym teacher, who has seen similar situations dozens of times.

Depending on the cause, there are several possibilities you might consider:

1. Have him privately coached in the sport's basic skills. If you can't do this yourself, it should be relatively easy to find a capable teenager—a member of the high school team, for example—who is willing to do so for a modest fee. The object is not to make your son into an Olympic athlete but merely to give him enough one-on-one instruction so that he will feel relatively comfortable with the game.
2. If he really is too awkward to participate as an athlete, help him find other ways to get involved. His goal is to belong and to share in his classmates' interests. Soccer teams need help with equipment, scorekeeping, scheduling, and so on. If your son volunteers for some of these responsibilities, then he'll be right there during the game and will be able to share in the excitement. How successful this approach will be depends to a large extent on the attitude of the team's coach. If he understands your son's situation and is sympathetic, the plan should

work. But if this is not true, the plan could backfire with your son becoming the object of ridicule. So the obvious first step is to meet with the coach and determine his attitude.

3. A slightly different approach is to encourage your son to become an armchair expert. Get him books on the sport so that he can become familiar with its history, its great players, its classic games, and its strategy and tactics. If he finds he is really interested in the subject, he'll soon be able to hold his own in any discussion of the sport.

4. Follow your wife's suggestion to get him involved in some other type of after-school activity. The disadvantage of this approach is that your son's peers are absorbed in soccer at precisely the age when peer relationships are critical, and finding another after-school activity will not solve the problem of your son's feeling left out at school. On the other hand, the problem is probably seasonal—the topic of conversation will change once the soccer season has ended.

Even though your son's basic self-esteem will not disappear overnight, you should discourage him from wallowing in negative feelings about himself. Motivate him to get out and participate to the best of his ability. You will see a much happier son.

Positive Attitude

My children love to make a surprise breakfast or lunch for me. I like the idea of their learning how to cook, but our deal is that they have to clean up the kitchen when they are finished. The problem is that the kitchen is never clean enough, so I end up angry with them; I have to spend time redoing what my children are perfectly capable of doing right themselves.

It must be hard for your children to plan on surprising and pleasing you, only to have it end up with your being angry. To view themselves as competent, your children need your encouragement. The next time they cook, surprise them with your praise over the parts of the kitchen that *were* cleaned to your satisfaction. Don't point out the things they missed. They will respond more to praise than to criticism and will try even harder the next time.

Parental Criticism

My son and husband have a very strained relationship. They don't actually argue much, but there is always an undercurrent of tension between them. My son is expected to so some chores around the house, and sometimes he forgets. Even when he does remember, his dad looks for something wrong with the way the chores were done and then starts to pick on him about other things, criticizing everything from his sloppy appearance to the fact that he had a C on his last report card. My son has seemed on edge with his dad since early childhood.

Perhaps your husband's parents treated him in precisely the way he is treating your son. He probably isn't aware of the dramatic impact this critical attitude can have on a child's self-esteem. Express your concerns to your husband in a way that does not attempt to place the blame on either party. Describe the tension you have observed and ask him to join you in searching for more effective solutions to problems. This pattern has become a part of your family life, and it is going to take a major family effort to break it.

You would be wise to look for help and support from books and community classes on effective parenting. If your husband is unable or unwilling to attend classes with you, bring home the ideas you have gathered and share them with him.

Be sure to include your son in the efforts to change the family dynamics. Describe the pattern you have seen and tell him how much you want things to change. Be honest with him about your feelings and explain that no one person is to blame. Encourage him to take his chores seriously, as their completion will prevent some friction.

Help your son compile a list of his good features.

Ask your husband to acknowledge these positive traits and to add a few more to the list. Children's feelings about themselves largely reflect the attitudes they see in their parents. It is essential that your son consider himself a worthy person in his parents' eyes.

Role Models

I have been a full-time homemaker since the arrival of my first child twelve years ago. We have a wonderful family of two boys and one girl. My husband and all of my brothers and sisters have been very successful in careers. Unintentionally, they have all helped me to believe that I have done little of which I can be proud. As a result, I put myself down and feel worthless and incapable in many ways. I was really upset when I recently heard my eight-year-old daughter talking with a friend. She said that she doesn't do anything really well and that she'll probably just be a housewife and mother when she grows up.

Children certainly take cues from their parents on how to view themselves. You and your daughter both need to change your outlooks. Being a housewife and mother is very demanding work. Many of the skills needed for top executive positions are also needed to run a household successfully.

You are the most important role model in your daughter's life. For her sake and yours, seek professional help.* You need to start valuing yourself. As you assess yourself and begin to realize how capable and successful you really are, you will begin to hold yourself in higher regard. At that point you will undoubtedly also see some positive changes in your daughter's attitude about herself.

Sibling Influence

My wife and I think we have the two greatest kids. We want them to feel good about themselves, but our ten-year-old son occasionally says very negative things to his six-

*See Appendix I.

year-old sister. Will her feelings about herself come primarily from us, or could her brother mess things up?

While parents are the most significant people in children's lives, siblings can have tremendous influence on each other. In many families, older children try to rule the roost, sometimes resorting to very nasty tactics. A great deal about relationships can be learned through sibling struggles. Naturally, your daughter can be influenced by her brother's attitude towards her. His messages to her—both verbal and nonverbal—certainly will affect her self-esteem.

Let your son know that you need his help with your daughter's developing self-concept. Praise his positive interactions with her; if you react exclusively to the negative interactions, then you'll fail to encourage the positive ones. Once or twice a week over dinner, ask each person at the table to repeat one nice thing he or she said to another family member during the past few days. If your son and daughter look forward to reporting the nice things that they said, their relationship will undoubtedly improve.

Plight of the Perfectionist

Our daughter is a success by anyone's standards. She earns good grades at school, she is the outstanding pianist at recitals, and she is always the star pupil at Sunday school. My husband and I always tell her that she's terrific, but she doesn't seem happy. She is quick to say negative things about herself and she sobs if she thinks someone might outperform her. We wish she would enjoy life more, but we don't know how to help her.

Regardless of the number of achievements, your daughter's self-esteem will not improve unless her attitude changes. Evaluate the feedback you give your daughter. You may well be praising the final results of her efforts and neglecting the process. If your daughter can learn to enjoy the activities for their own sake and place less emphasis on final results, she might begin to derive more satisfaction and feel better about herself.

CONCLUSION

A sense of self is not instinctive. It is gradually learned, and it is greatly influenced by parental attitudes. An appreciative attitude toward a new baby's existence is the best welcome a parent can offer. No matter how much parents want their children to feel good about themselves, children sometimes do feel inadequate. Because self-image continually shifts, parents need to help their children deal with negative feelings.

Parental approval, acceptance, and love are essential to self-approval, self-acceptance, and self-love in a child. Whether children form constructive or destructive attitudes toward themselves and others depends largely on their parents' attitudes toward them. A sense of autonomy, the inner knowledge that one is capable and successful in the world, is the cornerstone of self-esteem. The next chapter looks at that subject.

CHAPTER 5

THE IMPORTANCE OF AUTONOMY

From early infancy, children realize that they can have an impact on the world: a baby cries, a parent responds; a little one stretches arms out and is picked up; a smile produces a smile. So many little routine happenings teach a baby about life. This slow, intricate process helps children to become unique individuals, separate and different from everyone else. Throughout this process, parents are crucial in helping their children achieve autonomy.

Autonomy is one of a child's most basic needs. It means an ability to act and react successfully in the world, a general feeling of self-reliance. Children learn to feel competent when parents provide daily opportunities for autonomous growth. The chapter "Helping Children Take Care of Their Bodies" suggested ways to encourage autonomy in the daily routines of eating, bathing, and getting dressed. Many of the things a child learns to do may appear simple, but each new accomplishment helps prepare the child for coping with the more complex challenges encountered later in life.

Parents must sense when a child is ready to begin working toward a new responsibility. Encouraging a child to try something long before he or she is ready leads to frustration and self-doubt. Waiting until the thing is too easy will rob the child of the satisfaction of conquering a challenge. Autonomy becomes addictive; the more responsibility children successfully handle, the more they want to assume. Children who are given appropriate responsibility view life as a series of exciting challenges. The examples that follow demonstrate some of the ways parents might encourage the development of autonomy.

Our four-year-old son likes to ask a number of questions about where we are going on a family outing. Then he plans his outfit accordingly. My husband doesn't like to delay our departure just because our son is still dressing and filling his pockets with trinkets he's convinced he'll need. My husband wants me to speed up the process by dressing our son. I think it is important for him to dress himself.

Taking Time

You and your husband are lucky to have a son who demonstrates such a high level of autonomy for his age. He seeks information about the outing and then tries to plan his outfit and accessories logically.

It is very important to refrain from doing for your son what he can do for himself. He will not feel capable if you dress him or rush him. Young children do not master skills without a lot of practice. You don't want him to give up or become dependent on adult help. The best thing you can offer him is your tolerant waiting, followed by praise for his accomplishments. You might also work with your husband to prevent a last-minute rush. Whenever possible, let your son prepare for the outing the night before. Give him time to ask his questions and set out all the things he needs. Encourage him to begin dressing long before it is time to leave. Let him know that it is all right to finish some of the final snaps, zippers, or buttons in the car. The initiative he is demonstrating must be nurtured and appreciated.

My parents always directed my life, and I think I'm making the same mistake with my daughter. I have trouble deciding simple things like what to wear or what to eat. However, I can easily tell my daughter what she needs to do, wear, or eat. Recently, I suddenly realized that she waits for my

Making Choices

directions before doing anything. I wish she would show some initiative, but I think I've taken it away from her.

Ideally, autonomy is fostered in children from birth, but it is never too late. It is a good sign that you recognize your mistake. Now you can begin to change your approach and foster independence rather than dependence.

You describe your daughter as incapable of making simple decisions. At least once a day, help her decide some things for herself. Present several equally good alternatives and let her think her decision through without hearing your opinion. It will be hard for you to withhold your comments, but you'll be glad you did. If your daughter tells you that she doesn't know how to go about deciding, help her weigh the possible consequences. She may need this kind of help to begin learning the basic process of decision making. Since you offered two good alternatives, whichever she selects will have a positive outcome.

Remember that there is more than one way to solve most problems. With time and practice, your daughter will develop confidence in her ability to make intelligent choices.

Decisions

Our son spends a lot of time with a boy his age who lives down the block. He often tells me that his friend gets to make a lot of decisions at his house. Personally, I think that a seven-year-old is too young to make a lot of decisions, but our son is envious. He constantly says we treat him like a baby.

Every family is unique. The rules for one family do not necessarily apply to another. However, we can become so caught up in hectic daily routines that we don't realize when our children are ready to accept new responsibilities. The next time your son complains that you are treating him like a baby, thank him for reminding you that he is ready to move forward. Encourage him to tell you when he feels that you are underestimating him. Let him know that we can all learn from observing others. Encourage him to keep gathering new ideas.

Together you can discuss the kinds of decisions he wants to make. Be sure to settle on areas in which you feel you'll be able to support his decisions. Your goal should be to assist your son in successful decision making. With your help, he'll have the necessary preparation to make independent decisions as an adult.

I have enjoyed juggling my life as a mother and business executive. Everything seemed to be going smoothly until a recent business trip. My six-year-old son was fine with his dad and the babysitter, but when I returned home the problems began. He follows me everywhere, like a shadow. When he has to go to the bathroom, he asks me to go with him. I used to do that when he was two, but it seems ridiculous now. How could he lose his independence when I was gone only a week? **Regression**

Many different things can trigger regression in children. An illness, the absence of a parent, and the death of a relative are some examples. Children revert to earlier behavior patterns in order to feel safe again. This behavior becomes alarming only when it persists for weeks or months.

Talk with your son about the trip you took. Encourage him to remember that he missed you and felt glad when you returned. Assure him that missing people is one of the difficult but wonderful parts of loving. Respect his need to regress, and do not ridicule him.

It is also important, however, to avoid confusing your son by giving him mixed signals about his self-reliance. Tell him clearly that you realize he is perfectly capable of going to the bathroom by himself. You might say that once in a while you will be happy to go with him but that you know he will soon not need any help.

Or you might tell him that while he goes to the bathroom you'll search for a good book to read with him when he is finished. This is a way to give him attention without being a bathroom escort service. Feel confident that his regression is understandable and temporary. His well-established independence will reappear.

Being Bossy

My five-year-old daughter is preoccupied with playing house. I enjoy hearing her assume all of the family roles with her friends, but whenever children refuse to play house with her, she tells them to go home and she means it. If they don't share her interest, she won't play with them.

There are both positive and negative aspects to this situation. Playing house is a good way for children to begin to acquire autonomy; as they play the roles of various household members, their perspective of the world begins to broaden. (A good example of this process is when the play mother scolds her play child for doing something the "mother" herself has been scolded for.)

On the other hand, bossing one's friends around is a good way to lose the friends. Your daughter must learn to compromise. You might tell her to strike a bargain with her friends—if they play house for fifteen minutes, she'll play whatever they want for fifteen minutes. You could also help make playing house more interesting by letting them make a concoction in the kitchen or wear grown-ups' clothing. Finally, arrange for some activities outside of the home where she can be with her friends in an atmosphere where playing house won't become an issue.

Breaking Large Tasks into Small Steps

What can I do about a seven-year-old who refuses to clean his own room? When I tell him to clean it, he goes in and fools around. When I put pressure on him, he ends up crying, and his room still isn't clean. He's a real pack rat; he saves everything that appeals to him. I know he's capable of cleaning up, but I don't know how to get him going.

You are undoubtedly right about your son's capabilities, but your approach needs to be changed. Facing all of the clutter in his room is probably too overwhelming and frustrating. You shouldn't set him up for repeated failure. Instead, help him learn to complete tasks successfully, step by step.

Survey the room with your son to figure out an approach to cleaning. You two might decide that one shelf at a time should be cleaned, or perhaps small sections would be a better route. Your son might prefer to work in categories, such as toys, clothes, books, and collections. Part of the process will be helping him to see how many different ways he can face this task. You might want to set up a chart for him that lists the various tasks. Ask him if he'll agree to complete two small tasks a day. He can check them off as he goes, noting his own progress. Praise his efforts every step of the way and offer a little help now and then.

Learning how to break large tasks into small steps can help your son in the future. Many homework assignments need to be broken down when an initial assignment seems overwhelming. This method provides a logical, manageable way to conquer chores and attain a sense of achievement.

I love being a mother more than anything I have done in my life. I hate to see my children rushing to grow up. When my daughter found out that her friend makes her own breakfast, she insisted on taking on the same responsibility. My other child discovered that his two-year-old pal uses the toilet, and now he wants me to throw his diapers away so that he can use the toilet too. I like taking care of my children, and I don't want their childhood to end too soon.

Holding Children Back

Your children are fortunate that you so enjoy your role as their mother. What you have to keep in mind is the importance of helping them strive for autonomy. Parents must determine appropriate times to transfer responsibilities to their children. Even when your children are grown and have established homes of their own, you'll still be their mother. For now, you need to encourage the sense of self-pride that comes from meeting the challenges of daily living.

As children grow, their capacity for independence grows too. It is important to watch for new opportunities for growth and to ask continually, "Is my child ready to do this without my help?" Your children are actively looking for new forms of independence; applaud and encourage their efforts.

Responsibility with Independence

Our daughter is ten. After several years of asking if she could play at the neighborhood park, she finally got my wife to consent. I had always thought it would be a good place for her to spend some after-school hours. My wife's rule is that our daughter must telephone if she isn't going to get home by four o'clock. So far, she has followed this rule even when she was going to be only a few minutes late. I think if she is allowed to go to the park alone, she should be able to come home when she's ready.

It is important for your daughter to know that her parents trust her with this level of independence. The telephone rule and your daughter's willing cooperation probably help reduce your wife's anxiety. Your daughter isn't objecting to this rule. Perhaps she is pleased to know that her well-being is important to her family. The responsibility of keeping track of time and calling when she's late will help her feel competent and considerate. Praise her for being such a responsible family member.

Temper Outbursts

We want our son to feel strong and know that he can stand on his own two feet. The problem is that he often becomes difficult to live with when he stands up to us. He gets so angry that he yells. Then he mutters nasty things under his breath, just loudly enough for us to hear. He also pouts and sometimes shuts himself in his room. I thought two-year-old temper tantrums were bad enough, but this nine-year-old rebellion seems worse.

Your son's expression of his feelings through verbal aggressiveness, moodiness, and withdrawal is all part of the normal process of growing up. He is trying to establish himself as a separate human being with his own free will.

Outbursts of temper in any form are difficult and draining for parents. Your son does not expect or even want you to feel good about his negative behavior. He is responsible for it, and your disapproval is reasonable. Work on not prolonging the negative feelings. Be sure to praise him when he finds more appropriate ways to express his anger and independence. Continue to help your son feel strong, and know that he will eventually stand successfully on his own.

My sixth-grade daughter has always loved her dance classes. She wants to add two more classes a week. I can afford the additional expense, but I can't leave work to take her to them three times a week. Some of her classmates take the bus, and she is begging me to let her go with them. I am worried that something might happen to her.

Requesting Independence

Your daughter is expressing a desire to be more independent. Make sure she understands that you don't consider her inadequate but that you are worried about potential danger. You need to determine whether or not your concerns are founded. Talk with other parents, school administrators, the bus company, and the police department about the safety of the route. If possible, take the same bus at the time your daughter would be riding to dance class. This investigation should give you enough information to make an informed decision.

If your investigation determines the bus ride to be safe enough, have some discussions with your daughter. Ask her what she would do if the bus were late, if she lost her bus money, if she missed the bus, or if someone bothered her during the ride. Discussing potential problems and possible solutions can prevent trouble. If your daughter seems prepared for those situations, you can feel confident that she is ready for greater independence.

Drifting Away from the Family

Our eleven-year-old daughter seems to be drifting away from the family. She spends a lot of time alone in her room or with her friends. Recently she confided to us that one of her friends tried smoking. We are really worried about the things that could happen. We wonder whether we should insist on her spending more time with the family or just leave her alone?

This is a natural time for your daughter to withdraw a little from the family. She is not isolating herself when she chooses to spend time with her friends. You shouldn't worry, as her behavior is normal for her age. Growing up and becoming independent involves separating from the family and identifying with friends.

When your daughter does spend time with all of you, be sure to let her know how much you appreciate her. Eventually she will probably want to spend more time with you. For now, it is important for her to be able to withdraw without feeling guilty.

You are fortunate that your daughter trusts you enough to confide some of her secrets. Keep those lines of communication open by letting her know that you care and can handle what she chooses to share with you. Let your daughter know how much faith you have in her ability to cope with any situation she may encounter. Let her know too that you are always available if she wants your opinions or advice.

CONCLUSION

This chapter suggested ways to help children grow, stretch, and become more independent. Autonomy is the ability to think and act independently. There is no particular age or stage when a child suddenly becomes autonomous. Instead, autonomy is achieved slowly, as children waver between their consuming need for parents and their drive for independence. A major goal for parents is to encourage this process by giving children as much independence as they can handle safely and constructively. Over and over again, parents need to let children experience themselves as effective decision makers, capable of thinking and acting successfully on their own.

CHAPTER 6

FAMILY ISSUES

Newly married couples face the task of integrating the differing roles and habits carried over from their families. They need to create a mutually acceptable environment for their own home. They need to look at their upbringings and decide which features of them they want to recreate for their children. Couples may have long, involved discussions about what their family life with children is going to be like. What actually occurs— the reality, as opposed to the dreams and plans—depends on many factors, including each child's personality, the influence of relatives and friends, and the parents' relationship with each other. Such stresses as financial pressures can dramatically affect family life. Each new child arrives with a unique personality and adds to the complexity of family relationships. Consequently, moving from theory into practice is often more complicated than anyone could have anticipated.

No formal training is required for parenthood. The only absolute prerequisite is physical maturation, which does not ensure emotional or intellectual readiness for parenthood. Many parents report feeling truly shocked when they first realized the commitment involved in raising children.

Through trial and error, we discover how to deal most effectively with our children at various ages and stages. As soon as we feel even slightly competent with one phase, our children seem to leap into an entirely different phase. The trial-and-error process quickly begins again.

While it is impossible to anticipate all of the various problems that the give-and-take of family life creates, this chapter covers some of the more common ones.

Only Child

My husband and I are happily married and adore our five-year-old son. My mother constantly nags me to have another child. She says it isn't fair to make our son be an only child, and that he will never learn how to share the spotlight or get along with other children. We really don't want another child, and some of my mother's comments really get to us.

You might want to tell your mother that this topic is no longer open to comment or conversation. You and your husband are the only two who can make this decision.

Because of not having to share the spotlight, many only children feel extremely well cared for and loved. Of course, your mother is right in saying that your son will not learn the lessons of sibling rivalry. However, there are many other ways that you can help him learn to share and get along with others. Seek out group experiences for him; sports, camps, and clubs all offer programs in which children can work and play together. If your son has cousins, plan to have him spend time with them. Relatives can widen the family circle. Let your son invite friends to spend the night at your home. You might even be willing to include one of his friends on a family trip. These involvements offer opportunities for companionship and practicing social skills. Most importantly, continue enjoying your happy family of three.

Sibling Rivalry

For the last few months, our nine-year-old daughter has been really hard to live with. She makes cutting, cruel comments to her little sister and sometimes to us. She is unpleasant most of the time. Our four-year-old is the opposite. She is funny and loving almost all the time. My

husband and I really enjoy spending time with her, but
we dread the conflicts when the two girls are together. The
other night our older one said, "I know you like my sister
better than me." Her matter-of-fact statement shocked us,
and we didn't know what to say.

You were probably speechless because of your daughter's insight. It is important for you to respond to her
as honestly as you can. Thank her for telling you what
she has been feeling. Acknowledge how hard the last
few months have been for all of you. Point out that
when two sisters are at such different emotional stages,
there are bound to be problems. Admit that right now
you find her behavior upsetting and unacceptable,
whereas her sister is going through a happy, loving
stage. Remind her that you had wonderful times with
her in the past and are looking forward to more in the
future.

Work together on a plan for reducing conflicts.
Perhaps, for example, each parent could occasionally
spend thirty minutes alone with one daughter and then
thirty minutes with the other. Each child could have
parental attention without the interference of sibling
conflict. Time alone with you, combined with your
acceptance of her feelings, might help your nine-year-
old to outgrow this negative stage more quickly.

Arguing

I have six children, and assigning chores is always a prob-
lem. No matter how I do it, each one always thinks the
others' jobs are easier. We spend lots of time arguing about
this, and the kids get really angry with me. If all the time
spent fighting were spent on the chores, the work would
be done in no time.

Sharing chores is an ideal way of easing the family
work load. Chores also can help children experience
a sense of family responsibility and teamwork. Successful completion of any task, even an unpleasant
one, can enhance a child's self-esteem.

Because you have been the one to assign chores,

the children have made you the target of their discontent. You need to remove yourself from that role. Let your children take over the assignment of the chores. Maybe family members could take turns doling out the jobs, making charts, and assuming general responsibility for this leadership task. There are many possible systems for the assignment of chores. One method is to write out every chore on a separate slip of paper and have the children categorize each chore according to difficulty. At the beginning of each week, each child can pick one chore from each category, so that he or she will have some easy and some difficult tasks. The slips of paper can be shuffled and upside down so that no one knows which chores he or she is selecting. When this is left to chance, no one can be blamed for the assignments. In addition, the weekly lottery should inject a little fun into the process.

Favoritism

I am the father of two very different sons. One is athletic and outgoing, while the other is artistic and very quiet. I have always participated in sports, and I love to be with people. Naturally, it is exciting to have a son who is a lot like me. My wife gets along really well with both boys. We are a little worried that our artistic son will feel left out of the relationship between his brother and me. We just seem to be interested in different things.

Because children can be so different, it is impossible to love each of them in exactly the same way. There are several things you might do to become more involved with your artistic son. As you read magazines or newspapers, clip articles for him about artists and art shows. Offer to take your son and a friend to a local show. Ask him some questions about his own artwork—how he achieved a certain effect, for example, or where he got the idea. If your family takes a trip, find out about the art museums in the cities you visit. There are many little ways to let your son know that you appreciate and respect his interests, even though they differ from yours.

This morning I had a spat with my ten-year-old son. It wasn't the first, and I'm sure it won't be the last. This afternoon I overhead him talking with a friend on the phone. He was saying that he really hates me and wishes I'd leave him alone. I have been depressed for hours. How can a child suddenly turn against his own mother?

Overreacting

Perfectly healthy and normal family members can feel love, hatred, appreciation, and resentment for each other, all within the same day. There is nothing wrong with feeling conflicting emotions about the people who are most important to us. When we accept the existence of this wide range of emotions in ourselves, we then can accept it in those we love.

Your son sounds like a perfectly normal human being who is reacting to his morning spat with you. Don't be surprised if he is in a happy, loving mood by dinnertime. It is fortunate that he is willing to share his feelings with a friend instead of letting them fester.

Do not allow this incident to damage your relationship with your son, and do not make him feel guilty about it. He is probably just coming to terms with the fact that his parents are not perfect. This is an important step in the process of becoming an emotionally mature person.

My wife and I both come from very affectionate families. We like the warm atmosphere that such affection creates. We kiss our four children hello and good-bye every day. We also give them, and each other, spontaneous pats and hugs from time to time, and the children do the same. The problem is with big family gatherings. Our children are stubborn about not wanting to hug and kiss all of their relatives. It's really embarrassing for my wife and me because everyone else shows affection.

Expressing Affection

Physical affection between family members is a wonderful form of communication, quite different from communicating with words. The closeness helps reduce the psychological distance between people and is a clear expression of love.

It is nice that your family is so close, but you should not force your children to be physically affectionate for the sake of social customs. All children need to know very clearly that their bodies belong to themselves. No one has the right to coerce or embarrass them into sharing their physical selves. Of course parents have the right to expect their children to be well mannered at family gatherings. The children can greet relatives with a friendly handshake, smile, or words, but they should not be urged to hug or kiss.

You and your wife are role models for your children. They obviously can see the warm way that you greet your relatives. If they feel comfortable enough with any of the relatives to imitate you, they will. It is essential that you respect your four youngsters as unique individuals in charge of their own minds and bodies.

Manners

My husband and I agree that we want our children to have good manners, but we don't agree on how to achieve this. He feels the children should relax and enjoy dinners with the family, not worrying about manners. However, when we eat out or have company, he wants them to have perfect manners. I think we should get in the habit of using good manners all of the time.

You both have important points. Your husband is right that your children should feel relaxed and comfortable at home. You are right that manners should be used constantly so that they become a natural part of daily living. However, every family meal should not become the occasion for a sermon about manners.

Learning to use good manners takes time; children cannot learn all the rules and regulations in a few weeks or even in a few years. Be patient, and teach by example. React to your children's good manners with delight and appreciation. Children usually enjoy pleasing their parents, and your pleasure will encourage their socially acceptable behavior.

To go along with your husband's idea of wanting mealtime to be relaxed and enjoyable, plan a special dinner. Make an announcement at breakfast or send every family member an invitation to a "meal without manners." Request that everyone break all the rules of etiquette throughout the meal. This dinner will undoubtedly be a time for laughter, discussion, and increased awareness.

Routines

Before we had children my husband and I used to have weekends full of adventure. No one could ever predict where we would be, because we'd just get in the car and take off; we didn't even know where we were going. Now that we have three children, weekends have become a problem. My husband insists that we all pile into the car but usually everything goes wrong within a short time. One of the children begins crying that a favorite teddy bear was accidentally left behind, another becomes hungry or nervous about not knowing where we are going, I run out of diapers for the baby. Our "fun" turns into a nightmare.

Your weekdays are probably predictable for your children. You follow a fairly similar routine day after day. This routine makes your children's world seem organized and helps make them feel safe. The dramatic shift on the weekends can create turmoil and emotional distress. Daily stability undoubtedly makes life smoother for everyone.

Perhaps you can wait until your children are older to take weekend jaunts. For now, why don't you try one- or two-hour adventures in which the children can participate by telling the driver which way to turn the car. Exchange child-care responsibilities with a friend or hire someone to babysit from time to time so that you and your husband can get away alone. Without the children, you can recapture the excitement of your former weekend adventures.

Traditions

When I was growing up we had a family tradition of a dress-up dinner every Sunday. My mother's family had the same tradition when she was growing up. My oldest daughter thinks the whole idea is silly and keeps asking to be excused from attending so that she can spend the time with her friends. I really look forward to having the whole family together for a special meal once a week, but maybe it is silly.

Many families have certain traditions that they look forward to and observe regularly. These traditions help reinforce their identity as a family and keep members close to one another. Some of the traditions center around meals, others around games, readings, or shared discussions. Whatever form family tradition takes, it is worth preserving. Do not label your Sunday dress-up meals as "silly." Continue to have and enjoy them. But don't force your daughter to attend if she refuses vehemently. Her negative reaction could spoil the event. In time, perhaps she'll miss being there as much as you miss her presence.

Illness in Grandparents

My children have always been very close to their grandfather. He has been hospitalized for several weeks, and we still don't know if he is going to live. I have been spending so much time at the hospital that the children have begun asking a lot of questions. I don't want to get their hopes up or frighten them. How can I respond? Children are not allowed in this hospital, so they can't visit him.

The children obviously realize that something serious is happening. Knowing the truth will relieve rather than increase their anxiety. In a way appropriate to each child's age, parents should answer any question about illness or death as directly and truthfully as possible. Imagining what is happening is far more frightening for children than dealing with the truth. The children should be given time to adjust to the idea that their grandfather is seriously ill and may die. This will spare them from the pain that occurs when one learns suddenly that a loved one is dead.

You could draw a diagram of the hospital room and show your children where Grandpa's bed is. If you take some photographs, the children can see the room. Reassure the children that all the people at the hospital are doing the best they can to help Grandpa get well again.

Suggest ways in which the children could bring a smile to Grandpa's face. They could draw pictures, make cards, or collect some family photographs to send to him. Perhaps they could talk with him on the phone or wave to him from outside the hospital. They could work on a "get well" tape recording of songs and messages for Grandpa. Any of these activities will help them express their concern and love and include them in the healing process.

Violence

Before we were married and for the first years of our marriage, I didn't realize what a violent temper my husband has. It didn't really show up until our children came along. He doesn't get mad often, but it's awful when he does. He swears, throws things, and hits us. An hour later he wants us to forget the whole thing and make up. He acts so sweet then that it's hard to believe he's the same person. I live in fear of the next blowup and try not to cause it.

Family violence is more common than people want to believe. It affects families from every walk of life. Some family members actually look forward to the outbursts because they are followed by make-up periods, during which everyone is nice to everyone else—the only periods of peace the family has.

Violence may result when external stresses interact with previously existing internal tensions. The added responsibilities of having children has undoubtedly been stressful for your husband. Until you had children, he was able to function without serious blowups. It is imperative for you to get some professional help. In the meantime, the tension is mounting in all of you. If you are living in fear of the next blowup, your children must be even more frightened. This kind of violence in the home can leave children emotionally scarred for life.

There are many ways to get help. Contact a mental health association, a department of social services, a therapist, a clergyperson, or a women's shelter. One of these people or institutions will know where your family can get the kind of help it needs. You have a responsibility to yourself, your children, and your husband to make your home a safe place for everyone.

Divorce

My husband and I haven't gotten along for quite a while. We even went for counseling, but it didn't help. We have been keeping our problems a secret from the children. Now we are planning a separation before the actual divorce, so we must tell the kids something. It's hard to figure out what to say. We both really care about our children, and we don't want to hurt them.

It is sad when families break apart. It also is sad and damaging to raise children in an atmosphere of continual discord. Even though you feel you have kept your marital problems a secret, your children undoubtedly sense that things are not right. It will probably be a relief for them to have you share as much of the truth as you feel you can.

You are wise to think through the important matter of how to prepare the children. The energy you spend on this will help them make an easier adjustment. Tell them that you have been trying to work your problems out and that you even asked a counselor to help you. Explain that even though parents can separate and get divorced, they never divorce their children. Make it clear that they did not cause your problems and that they cannot get you back together. Tell them that these are grown-up problems.

If possible, separate temporarily within your own home. The concept of separation, when explained in words, may not be clear to them, but when they see you are no longer sharing a room, they will begin to get the idea. Encourage them to ask questions and to express their thoughts and feelings. Let them know how sad and sorry you are that things didn't work out. Communicate your conviction that things are going to be better, although not immediately.

Once one of you has actually moved out, take

your children to see where that parent will be living, and work out a visitation plan. It is imperative for your children to know that their contact with this parent will continue. Give your children clear permission to continue loving both of you. All of this talking, planning, and reassuring will help to reduce your children's fears of abandonment.

Fortunate are the children whose parents can set aside their differences and work together for a smooth divorce. This cooperative effort can help children adjust to the transitions of separation, divorce, and new living patterns. In the process of trying to convince their children that everything will work out, parents often convince themselves as well.

Single-Parent Dating

I have been divorced for three years. Until now, my children have been nice to the few men I have brought home. I finally met a man whom I like very much, and we are talking about the possibility of getting married some day. After I told my children that, they have been horrible to him. I thought they would be happy for me, so their behavior is a shock.

Most children spend a lot of energy vying for their parents' attention. For three years, your children have not had to compete with their father for your time. Perhaps your new friend is viewed as a serious competitor. They also may have been secretly wishing that you and their father would work things out and you'd all be a family again.

You have indicated that no definite marriage plans have been made. For now, it might be wise to stop discussing "some day" and just let your children get to know your friend. Remind them of how they have always been nice to new friends and tell them how pleased you are when people get to know them. Finally, find time to spend alone with them and continue the good relationship you have.

Stepparents

I've recently become the father of two children from my

wife's first marriage. We get along pretty well, but I've noticed that whenever they need something they ask their mother. I am capable of giving a great deal of myself and like the idea of being a parent. It hurts to have them reject my offers of help and always go to their mother.

When parents remarry, children frequently feel that the stepparent is invading their lives. A marriage certificate doesn't instantly change a group of adults and children into a family. It takes time, sometimes years, for the human relationships involved to run smoothly.

It is natural for your stepchildren to seek help from their biological parent. Give them time to get used to your being a part of their daily lives. At this point they might consider it disloyal even to ask for your help. Turning to their mother is a tried and true method of getting help. Without being pushy or overly helpful, look for subtle ways to be involved. When it is obvious that they want help but their mother isn't around, you could offer yours. You might say, "Your mother will be back in a few minutes. What's up?" If they aren't ready to accept your help, they will wait for her. When they *are* ready, they'll let you know. You might ask your wife to deflect some of their problems to you. When it seems appropriate, she can tell them she is too busy to help and that you will, or that you're better at that sort of thing (their spelling lesson, perhaps) than she is. Remember to be receptive, patient, and caring. They will spontaneously ask for your help in time.

CONCLUSION

Whether you are a single parent, a married parent, or a stepparent, you are part of a family. Parents are entrusted with the important task of raising children. During the early years of their lives, children are totally dependent. The family must provide protection, nurturing, financial security, and education. The family helps children adapt to society. A goal of the parenting process is to move children from dependence to successful independence. Ideally, each family member takes pleasure in being a part of this process.

When the goals seem so clear and parents have the best intentions, why does raising children often seem so difficult and overwhelming? Why can't life be like it is on television where families solve unbelievably complex problems in only thirty minutes? Why does it take us days to solve seemingly simple ones? The answer, of course, is that the characters on television are puppets manipulated by writers, directors, and actors, while we and our children are human beings—unique individuals who do not fit into preconceived molds. All too often, we feel embarrassed to discuss our problems with friends or relatives, because we think we should know what to do. We set high goals for ourselves and then feel inadequate when we don't reach them.

We need to stop expecting perfection from ourselves and our children. A more realistic goal is to continually increase our effectiveness in resolving the family problems that inevitably arise.

CHAPTER 7

DISCIPLINE

Discipline is one of the most difficult areas of child rearing. Parents encounter discipline situations at least daily and sometimes every few minutes. Your attitude toward discipline sets the emotional tone for the family. Your approach to discipline and the way you carry it out will have tremendous impact on how your children feel about themselves. Consequently, it is worth spending time and energy to create your own viable approach to effective discipline.

The most basic question to ask is what is the goal of discipline? You have to know what it is you are trying to accomplish and where you hope to go in order to determine how to get there. It is simple to agree that *self-discipline* is the ultimate goal of discipline. As children come to rely on their own behavior and inner controls, they are acquiring self-discipline. It is much harder to agree on how to help children develop self-discipline. The ideas in this chapter will help you see how to promote the growth of self-discipline in your children.

Is discipline for punishment or for change? We want our children to change, moving from misbehavior to self-controlled, appropriate actions and interactions. Punishment usually consists of adults doing something to children in an attempt to enforce established, rigid, adult rules. This approach to punishment is counterproductive—it encourages our children to test limits and, behind our backs, break the rules. Our children might behave when we are around just because they want to avoid our punishments and fear the repercussions of their misbehavior. When away from us, however, they might pursue the inappropriate behavior.

It is the authoritarian parent who does something *to*—rather than *with*—children. Such parents use their size and authority to intimidate their children. An authoritarian attitude brings out punitive characteristics in parents as they attempt to impose their will through threats, confrontations, moralizing, oppression, overpowering, and the generation of fear.

Some parents, without realizing the consequences, try to be their child's friend. These parents often feel helpless, unprepared, and unsure of themselves. They look the other way when their children are acting up and try to pretend it isn't happening. Other times they laugh at misbehavior, thinking this will please their child. It is confusing to young people, who are growing and testing limits, to find out there really are no limits. These children could have difficulty in school—and, later, in the community—when they are expected to adhere to rules and regulations. These same parents act shocked when their child's teacher or principal calls to report unacceptable conduct. These parents, themselves immature, repeatedly side with their child, claiming the teacher or another child is at fault. Because these children do not have respect for rules, they do whatever they wish and feel certain that their parents will defend them.

Abdicating one's role as a parent is not an effective solution. Parents who are too extreme, whether very strict or very lenient, often wonder why it is so difficult to be a parent. We must find a middle ground where we recognize and accept the powerfulness of our roles in raising children. Then we have to figure out ways to constructively help children discover how to use their own positive power.

We want to encourage a cooperative spirit between ourselves and our children. If we view discipline as something we do *with* children, then we need to identify the interactions between adult and child that will help bring about constructive change. A list of these interactions might include some or all of the following: guiding the children, exploring choices with them, acting as a team, learning together, negotiating differences, compromising, and maintaining mutual respect. This process of interaction should begin as early as possible, although it is never too late. If we work out family rules *with* children instead of *for* children, they will have more meaning.

Misbehavior occurs intermittently throughout childhood as a necessary part of testing limits and learning acceptable behavior. Typically, parents groan and feel the tension rising over each new power struggle. These situations are viewed as "problems" and they create frustration, dismay, and anger. Since we know that every day and, most likely, every hour will present another discipline situation, wouldn't it help to look forward to these moments as challenges to be the best parent we can? Undoubtedly, we will face a challenge with a far more optimistic outlook than we would face a problem.

One last, and important, question to ask ourselves is this: *Are we treating our children in ways we hope they will treat us and their peers?* If we can look back at a discipline situation that has been resolved and feel proud of our conduct and pleased with the parent-child interaction, then the answer is "yes"—we are acting as positive role models. This is the single most important thing we can do for our children.

What, then, is discipline? Discipline should be looked upon not as a means to control a child, but as a means to create self-control within the child; it is best achieved through an interaction between child and adult in which the adult provides guidance and serves as a model. When parents have a clear idea of the goal of discipline, the inevitable day-to-day incidents become opportunities or challenges for facilitating learning and change. Children need help in acquiring values and learning to control themselves. As children develop self-discipline, they learn that they can depend on themselves to act in appropriate ways. This leads to emerging positive self-esteem, a basic ingredient for a satisfying life. The suggestions in this chapter, like others throughout *Guideposts for Growing Up*, demonstrate that discipline is something parents need to do *with* (not *to*) children.

Troublemaking

My daughter leaves kindergarten at noon, but my son stays at school the whole day. Yesterday I stopped at the store after picking up my daughter. When I finished with my errand, we bought ice cream cones to eat on the way home. During the drive, my daughter gleefully said that her brother would be really upset when he found out we had ice cream. Why couldn't she just enjoy the treat instead of working on a plan to upset her brother?

Your daughter's behavior is a typical example of a perfectly normal condition—sibling rivalry. However, knowing how normal it is probably doesn't make it any less annoying for you. The next time that a similar situation arises, give your daughter a response she doesn't anticipate. Tell her how glad you are that she thought about her brother's being left out of the treat. Suggest that when you get home she can draw a picture of an ice cream cone and you'll write out a coupon for him that will be good for one cone. Tell her how happy you think her brother will be that she thought about him.

With this approach, you can turn a potentially negative situation into a positive one. Although your daughter's original plan—to torment her brother—will have failed, she will see that constructive actions have the double advantage of winning not only your attention but also your praise. If you continue to encourage positive behavior, there will be less discord in your family.

The other night, my sons were in the kitchen eating dinner together. I heard them giggling, but I didn't think much about it. When I went out there, I couldn't believe my eyes. They had used their forks and spoons to flip food at the ceiling. The kitchen looked like a disaster area. I was furious and sent them to bed without letting them watch their favorite television shows. It took me hours to clean up the mess.

Logical Consequences

If you thought about it, you could probably recall some of the really naughty things you did as a child. It seems to be part of growing up. You certainly had cause to be furious, but your punishment did not suit the crime. What did the lack of television and going to bed have to do with the mess in the kitchen? Boys who are handy enough to flip food to the ceiling are certainly handy enough to clean up their mess. They should have been put to work with buckets and sponges. They probably couldn't have gotten the place completely clean, but a major effort would have sufficed. The next time they felt like flipping food, they would be deterred by their memories of the hard work of cleaning up.

This use of logical consequences does not require a lot of emotional energy on the part of parents, and it makes sense to children. Always try to link punishment to a logical or a natural outcome. This will help you choose the most appropriate type of discipline for the situation.

**Innocent Until
Proven Guilty**

*The other day I called home from work and asked my
daughter to take the casserole out of the refrigerator and
put it in the oven at 325 degrees. I also asked her to set
the table. When I came home the table was only half set.
The casserole was in the oven, but the oven hadn't been
turned on. My daughter wanted to explain what had happened, but I just screamed at her. Every time she has tried
explaining, I've told her I don't want to hear. Just the
reminder makes me start screaming. I don't ask much of
my daughter, but I do expect her to pitch in when I make
such a simple request.*

You certainly have the right to expect your daughter
to follow through with your requests; however, she
has the right to be considered innocent until proven
guilty. You still don't know why the two simple chores
weren't done: your daughter has been denied the
chance to explain. If her reason really was valid, perhaps you would have understood. What if something
dangerous had happened? Perhaps smoke began
pouring out of the oven a few minutes after she turned
it on. Or perhaps she received a disturbing prank call
and was so upset that she called a friend or relative
for help. There are many possibilities. Of course, she
may simply have become preoccupied. The important
thing is to reserve judgment until you are sure she let
you down. If you deny her the chance to discuss what
happened, then you are saying that her thoughts, feelings, actions, and reasons don't matter. This will hamper her chances for building a healthy level of self-
respect.

Remaining angry for hours or days, screaming,
and trying to keep the other party feeling guilty is not
the sort of behavior that you want to hold up as a
model for your daughter. Learning how to resolve conflicts and move on is an important aspect of living.
You will enjoy life and being a parent a lot more if
you can find more effective ways to communicate.

Rebellion

*Our eleven-year-old son has been easy to raise until now.
This once neat and well-dressed boy has been coming to*

the dinner table in dirty and torn clothes. We can handle it in our own home, but this weekend he actually thought we'd take him to a restaurant when he was dressed like that. We're embarrassed at the thought of going out with him when he looks such a mess.

Sometimes young people go through phases of trying to make statements through their appearance. Maybe his friends are dressing the same way. He might simply be testing your parental authority, using his clothes as his form of rebellion. If you do take him out with you, he might notice the stares or hear the comments of others and feel embarrassed enough to dress appropriately the next time. If you are too uncomfortable to take him out in dirty and torn clothes, then tell him so. Give him plenty of time to clean up when you are planning to go to a restaurant. If he doesn't want to change, tell him matter of factly that he can check the refrigerator for something to eat, and then leave without him. It is important to make it clear that you are not punishing him but giving him a choice. Save the emotional battles for more serious issues, as this phase probably will not last long.

When our children misbehave I let them know I'm furious. Then I don't talk to them for a few hours or even a few days. My husband thinks it's wrong, but the way they fought over a toy yesterday made me so angry that I really don't want anything to do with them.

Parental Withdrawal

Children's fights can be tremendously disturbing. However, when children are acting their worst, they really need their parents' help. By tuning them out you are letting them know that your parental involvement is conditional: if they behave you'll be there for them, but if they misbehave you'll withdraw and ignore them. Pretending they don't exist is a form of emotional abuse, and that is certainly not your intention. You have probably already learned that walking away with your anger doesn't change your children's behavior and it doesn't leave you feeling very effective.

Tell your children that you are going to try to express your feelings consistently. Let them know that sometimes you can't stand their behavior but you still value them. Keep in mind that you do not want to destroy your relationship with them or crush their spirit. Instead, guide them and show them better ways of resolving differences.

It might be helpful to take a parent-education course* or to read some books on discipline. If you are determined, you will find some new approaches for handling typical altercations between siblings. You will learn to get involved and feel more effective as a parent and as a person.

Whining

My daughter has a habit of whining in a way that sends chills down my spine. The worst thing is that yesterday I heard myself whining right back at her. I've probably done it a hundred times before, but I never realized it.

Your daughter's annoying habit has elicited an immature, childish response from you. Your recognition will help you to stop whining and find more effective responses. In all likelihood your daughter has been getting immediate attention for her whining, which tends to encourage it. Even though she might not like the kind of attention she receives, she has you as her captive audience.

Find a time when you are both in good moods to discuss this problem. Tell her how intensely you dislike her whining and how shocked you were to discover that you also whine. Mention an adult you know who whines to point out that this habit can go on for a lifetime. Tell her that it's a childish and annoying form of communication and that you can help each other stop. Ask her to let you know the minute she hears you whine so that you can try to stop it. If you hear yourself start whining, stop in the middle of a

*Such courses are offered in many areas by community colleges, high school adult-education programs, YMCAs, or church groups. The public library is often a source of information about the availability of these courses.

sentence and talk about what you just heard yourself do and how much you want to break the habit. You will be seeking your daughter's help while displaying your own determination. Pick times to review how each of you is doing. Plan to have a celebration when you both have succeeded in breaking the habit. Your daughter has received so much negative attention for whining that it is very important to give her positive attention for conquering this annoying habit.

No matter what goes wrong in my son's life, he always has the perfect excuse. He blames someone or something else for everything. He is constantly on the go, so my best chance to talk with him is just before he falls asleep at night. Somehow our talks never turn out the way I'd hoped. He usually ends up crying and upset with me and yells that I blame him for things he didn't do.   **Excuses**

Fatigue affects human perception and, consequently, communication. After a long day of work or play, the most simple problems may appear insurmountable. When people are tired, they tend to be more emotional than rational.

You describe yourself as continually engaging your son in serious discussions when he is tired. You can probably avoid the tension, tears, and hostility by simply delaying important topics until morning. A good night's sleep can go a long way toward eliminating emotional confrontations. Talk with each other when you are rested and relaxed, perhaps over breakfast before he's become involved in the day's activities.

You are right to want your son to take responsibility for his own behavior. The way that you approach him will help determine the success or failure of your effort. When a child is quizzed in an angry or an accusatory manner, it is likely that he or she will deny any wrongdoing. If children fear harsh punishment or their parents' rage, it becomes safer to offer an excuse. When children get in the habit of placing blame on something or someone else, they eventually begin to believe their made-up stories.

If you already know that your son is responsible for causing a problem, ask him about it in a nonthreatening, nonpunitive way. Let him know that you want to help him work out a solution. Your goal should be to help him discover acceptable ways to resolve problems. In the long run, this skill will be far more useful than excuses. You will help your son feel able to conquer the inevitable problems that everyone must face.

Hitting Children

When my daughter hits her younger brother, I really let her have it. I want my kids to know right from wrong. When I was growing up I knew that my father would pull out his belt and let me have it if I didn't behave—and that's how I learned right from wrong. My wife thinks kids shouldn't be hit. Who is right?

Many parents get angry enough to lose control and hit their children sometimes. As a regular method of discipline, however, this is not effective. Children clearly learn from their parents' actions. You are doing exactly what your father did to you, and you are teaching your own children that it is all right to strike someone in anger. If it is wrong for your daughter to hit her brother, how can it be right for you to hit her? If you want her to use her words instead of her fists, you are going to have to start using words as well.

Switching methods of discipline is not easy. You may need to seek professional help* to assist you in changing the pattern that you have lived with for many years. It will, however, be worth the effort. You will feel proud of yourself, and your children will benefit.

Repetitive Fights

My seven- and nine-year-old boys constantly fight over which TV shows to watch. I can't stand these battles and think the best solution might be to get rid of the television set.

*See Appendix I.

You are describing the kind of repetitive fights many siblings have. Undoubtedly, the television set is not the only cause of their disagreements. Getting rid of it may be your way of saying you give up, but similar problems will have to be solved sooner or later. If you warn your sons that you will give the television set away if they continue fighting, be sure you are willing to follow through. Children quickly learn to identify hollow threats, and you will lose your credibility if you back off.

Battles over the TV set offer excellent opportunities to demonstrate ways of resolving conflicts. It is important for your boys to know that you dislike their repetitive fighting and consider them capable of working out their problems. Children of their ages are especially concerned with the principle of being fair, and suggesting possible solutions that appeal to their sense of fair play might be the way to solve the problem. One approach would be to put each one in charge of picking TV shows every other day. Another way would be to have each child pick his favorite shows and list their times. Where there are conflicts, one child will get to make the choice during one time period and the other child during the next time period; the next day, the order will be reversed. You might want to tell them that if they cannot work out a cooperative, fair schedule and they continue to fight, then you will turn the TV off until another day when they can try again. If they come to understand that you mean what you say, they might prefer to work out their problems. If they do continue to fight, they'll probably be wise enough to do it quietly.

Ruined Dinners

Our four-year-old son is unable to sit still for five minutes, and he manages to ruin every family meal. He tumbles off his chair, crawls under the table, and wanders around the room. My husband says it isn't worth trying to have dinner with him, but I don't think we should give up so easily. I have told our son over and over again that his behavior at the dinner table is unacceptable. Although he's a bright boy, my words seem to make no difference.

Any time you find yourself doing the same thing "over and over again," accept the fact that your approach is ineffectual. You need to find ways to make family dinners more pleasant.

Because your son is only four, making dinner as brief as possible will help to ensure his success at behaving properly. At each meal, praise him when he displays appropriate behavior. "We are so pleased you are sitting still and talking with us," you might tell him. Your positive comments will allow your son to experience praise, rather than constant complaints. If your son seems to be losing control, ask him if he would like to finish his meal standing up. Four-year-olds often have so much energy that sitting for even a short period is too much to expect. Allow your son to excuse himself from the table when he is finished. Let him know that you expect him to occupy himself until everyone else has finished eating.

Tell your husband what you plan to do so he can cooperate. Then tell your son that something new is going to happen at dinner tonight, something that will make dinnertime happier for the whole family. Briefly explain your new ideas, and tell him you're sure that he will be a cooperative family member. Let him know that after dinner you will play a family game to celebrate the successful dinner. By telling him in advance, you'll give him a chance to think about his new role.

If your son excuses himself before you've finished eating, assure him that it will only be a few minutes until you will play the family game. Approach this whole plan with the conviction that it is going to work. Your positive attitude will affect your son's success.

Spitting

When our six-year-old son gets angry he spits at anyone who says something he does not want to hear. His victims have been both children and adults. Once he even spit at his teacher, and she sent him to the principal's office. It has been difficult to find a punishment that will stop his spitting. To make matters worse, our two younger children have begun acting the same way. The whole thing is disgusting and embarrassing.

It is understandable that you find spitting intolerable. Think about how you have tried to solve this problem; it might be helpful to ask yourself what you think discipline is. Then, ask yourself if you are using discipline to *punish* or to *change*. Of course you want change, but often punishments do not create change. Punishments can create fear, and fear might succeed in stopping a certain kind of behavior. But fear also can make children become sneaky to avoid getting caught. Your goal must be to help your son change through gaining self-control.

Some day when your son has not been involved in a spitting incident and seems to be in a receptive mood, sit down and have a brief talk with him. Ask him if he really understands why spitting is unacceptable. Explain how spit can spread germs and discuss this and other reasons why people consider spitting to be abusive or antisocial behavior. You don't want to sound punitive, so it's important to speak in a voice that is not harsh. You want to talk *with* your son, not *at* him. Point out that the younger children admire and imitate him, and that you are concerned because they are copying his spitting habit.

Tell him there are two places where it is okay to spit: the toilet and the bathroom sink. Explain that if he feels upset enough to spit, he can move away from the people who are making him mad and run to the bathroom to spit. There he can spit as much as he wants without people getting mad at him, and he won't get germs on anyone. Be sure to tell his teacher (or let your son tell the teacher) about this new plan.

Let your son know that you love him and want to help him behave so that other people aren't constantly angry with him. Ask him to think of things he can say or do when people make him angry; discuss possible choices and guide him toward acceptable ones. One of the best ways for him to really learn something is to teach it; the next time one of your younger children spits, call for your six-year-old and ask him to show his brother or sister where it is okay to spit. Making him the resident expert on spitting will also have the positive effect of putting him in a constructive leadership role. Your constructive intervention will be for change, not for punishment, and it may result in some very positive feelings by your son.

Rejecting a Parent   *Our three-and-a-half-year-old daughter always prefers me, which makes her father feel left out and hurt. I discourage her from acting this way, but it just seems to happen. I'm worried that this is having a negative impact on our family life. There was a horrible scene the other night because her dad wanted to help her with her nightly bath. When she wanted me instead, her dad went into a rage and screamed, "Just go to bed without a bath!" She cried for a long time. This kind of scene is happening every few days.*

Perhaps your daughter spends more time with you than with her father. Whatever the reason, it is normal for children to bond more closely with one parent than the other at certain ages and at certain stages in their development. Your husband may feel excluded from the close relationship between you and your daughter. When she blatantly rejects him, it is more than he can handle. Feeling left out and rejected, he then loses his temper.

The missed bath won't harm your daughter's body, but the outbursts of rage could damage her emotional well-being. Since your daughter is too young to understand this problem, you must find ways for you and your daughter to let your husband know how important he is within the family unit. Be sure that you and your husband get away for some evenings alone. You don't want your husband to feel that you prefer your daughter's company to his.

Your daughter will be able to make her dad feel more secure if you guide her in planning father-daughter events and activities. For example, "surprises for Daddy" might consist of a painting on the door to welcome him home or homemade muffins that she can present to him at dinner. Select some of her favorite books and put them on a "Daddy shelf." Whenever she wants those books read to her, she will have to ask her father; only Daddy can touch the things on his shelf. Later, games and other toys might be included on this shelf. Of course, your daughter will need to seek her father's company to enjoy them. As the father-daughter relationship grows in a positive direction, you will know it is worth the planning and effort.

Tearing

I talked on the phone for 15 minutes with no interruptions from our son. It was a mistake not to check on him. When I went in the living room, he was looking quite pleased because he had torn one of his books into shreds. I wanted to let him know that I was really really angry, but couldn't figure out what to do, so I sent him to his room. Do I have to keep our books beyond his reach to protect them?

You didn't mention your son's age, but even young children should help with the clean-up process after making a mess. Keeping his books under lock and key will protect them. However, this would only protect the books within your home; he could still destroy books at school, the library, or at friends' homes. You need to find an effective way to let your son know what is unacceptable behavior. The book you mentioned was torn beyond repair. If it could have been fixed, having him help would have been a good beginning. You might refuse to read to him for a few days and insist that he stay away from any books in your home.

Locate an outdated telephone book and put your son's name and even a photograph of him on the cover. Show him the difference between the family phone book that is used as a directory and the old one that you have designated as his. Explain that because people move and get new phone numbers, the telephone company gives away new books every year. Rather than throwing your old directory away, you are giving it to him for wherever he feels like tearing pages. Sit by a wastebasket and explain that he can throw out the torn-up sheets as he goes along or when he is finished, but when he is through everything must be cleaned up. Having his own phone book should channel his tearing energy.

Difficult Transitions   *I have been divorced for several years. My three- and five-year-old children both have a hard time leaving when their dad comes to pick them up. One sets the other off, and they both start crying and clinging to me. It usually ends up with me dragging them to his car. When they finally leave, I am emotionally exhausted. Then I have to brace myself for their return the next day after they have spent the night at his apartment. They usually return home tired and in terrible moods. It's impossible to get them tucked into bed without tears and angry words. So far, I can't figure out what to do. When I try to talk to their dad, he says the children are just fine when they are with him. When our normal routine is resumed, everything goes smoothly.*

Transitions from your house to their father's and back again are creating emotional turmoil. Ask their father for his help in finding solutions to this challenge. Perhaps you could meet at a park and let them begin playing with their dad before you say good-bye. Another approach, if you're comfortable with it, would be to invite your ex-husband in to visit with the children before they leave. Just a short visit of 5 or 10 minutes could help to make a smoother transition. Children often feel emotionally torn in divorce situations. The two of you can help them learn to accept the divorce as a reality and to cope more effectively with it.

When their dad brings them back, games can provide a transitional activity that will catch their attention and make things easier. You could leave a sign on the outside door for their dad to read to them. It could say, "Try to find me, I'm hiding in the room that has the most food." As soon as they find you, give one of the children a chance to hide and you and your other child will be the search party. Another idea is to tell them when they return to hurry along with you to get ready for bed because there is a surprise waiting for each of them. You know your children and what would be a nice surprise for them, so just plan ahead. You will be taking the focus off their transition problems and onto something to look forward to.

It is difficult to have a constructive conversation

about emotional issues when children are tired. When your children are rested, remind them of the crying and fighting they used to have when they came home. Point out what a pleasant ending you all had the night before when you played the hide-and-seek game. Assure them you will plan something for the next time they come back from their dad's. All of this takes more effort on your part, but it's far less exhausting than the negative transitions.

Our family went to a movie last weekend. I was distressed to find that a "family" movie showed the leading man acting in extremely disrespectful ways toward women. There was no physical violence, but the actor ordered the women around as if they were dirt. Yesterday my son tried the same thing with me, demanding something in a commanding, disrespectful tone. I was shocked and speechless, and didn't do what he wanted. I assume my son was imitating what he saw in the movie.

Verbal Abuse

You are probably right with your assumption that this behavior was a direct result of the movie. Research has shown that movies and television shows can have a tremendous impact on the outlook of children. Each character and every interaction provide models that children often follow. After the release of a particularly violent movie or the airing of a violent television show, it is not uncommon to read in the news about numerous copycat acts of violence.

Think about the audience reaction to the scenes you disliked. If the audience laughed or whistled, your son would be encouraged to think an abusive way of relating is acceptable.

Did you and your husband discuss the movie with your children on the way home? Did you talk about the parts that you thought were inappropriate for a family-rated movie? The next time this happens, tell your children that you objected to some scenes and ask them to guess which ones you disliked and why. As a family, you can then discuss what was wrong, helping your children to recognize the undesirability of transferring the movies's negative aspects into real life. By participating in this type of activity while the movie is fresh in the children's minds, you could prevent the situation from recurring.

You said that you were "shocked and speechless." If, after you calmed down, you did not discuss the incident with your son, you could bring it up even weeks later. You need to be sure he understands how demeaning his attitude was. The next time you decide to go to a "family-rated" movie, tell your children they should watch and listen for things that are inappropriate and agree to not imitate them. If this behavior happens again, leave the offending child or children at home the next time you go to a movie. Parents are responsible for teaching their children acceptable behavior, and you want to do everything possible to help your children become constructive, caring people.

Incentives

We have only three children in our family, but if anyone heard the bickering and fighting that goes on, they would think we have at least a dozen. The other night I couldn't stand it any more, and I told my husband I was prepared to pay the children to stop these horrid scenes. He was upset over the idea and feels we shouldn't bribe our children to behave. I asked him if he could think of a better way, but he couldn't. The yelling continued, and then my husband and I started snapping at each other. I would still like to try paying the children to stop fighting just so we could have some peace and quiet once in a while.

Constant bickering, shouting, and turmoil at home can leave people with a feeling of continuous exhaustion. It is no wonder that the relationship between you and your husband has become strained. You not only have to listen to the children's irritating behavior, but you also disagree on how to change it. The important thing is to begin experimenting with ways to help your children change. Ongoing turmoil can lead to a dysfunctional family, one in which emotional and social growth is hindered.

Rather than pay your children to stop bickering,

offer them incentives to do so. Explain to your husband that the difference between an incentive and a bribe, although subtle, is extremely important—an incentive is a reward for success, not a payment to stop failure. Many business corporations use incentive plans to increase the productivity of their employees; upper management does not consider gifts, trips, or bonuses to be "bribes" but as means to motivate the work force to achieve its maximum potential. The same principle can apply to family situations.

Young children, of course, are not very interested in money. Most children, young or old, are interested in toys and in simple objects that can become their treasures—a pin, perhaps, or a special article of clothing. Determine in advance how much to spend and take the children to one or two stores to select things for a treasure chest. Tell each child the exact number of items that he or she will be allowed to pick. Be sure to keep each child's treasures in a separate bag within the treasure chest. As a family, decide how many hours they will have to get along without bickering before they can earn something from their bags. At first, agree to a relatively short period of time so the children experience early success. As their behavior begins to improve, you can negotiate longer and longer intervals. You and your husband will be constructively helping them to develop one of the most important goals in life—inner controls, or self-discipline. As parents, you will probably experience a sense of satisfaction and the daily joy of some harmonious hours in your home.

Fighting Friends

I am a single father who has joint custody of my son. I pick him up from the day-care center several times a week, and he spends the night at my apartment. Last week he begged to have his best friend come home with him. I am tired at the end of my work day, and it is an effort to get my son fed, bathed, and to sleep; I couldn't imagine dealing with his friend, too. Nevertheless, I finally agreed to have his friend over on Saturday for lunch and the afternoon. Unfortunately, the visit turned into a nightmare. The boys fought and screamed about everything, acting more like enemies than friends. After three hours of this, I phoned the friend's house to ask his mother to pick up her son earlier than planned, but no one was home. So I had to put up with another two hours of torture. Believe me, it will be a long time before my son can invite a friend over again.

I'm not sure who is responsible for the problem. I told my son that he must prove to me that he is capable of getting along with a friend before we'll try that again.

You didn't mention your son's age, but you did say he is in day-care. This means he probably is between two and five years old. Few children within this age group can get along with another child for five consecutive hours. The next time a friend is going to visit, limit the get-together to a maximum of one-and-a-half hours and be prepared to spend the entire time supervising their activities. You must keep an eye on them to decide when an activity needs to be changed or stopped, and you have to prevent the boys from becoming so excited that their emotions get out of control. Young children need adults to help them learn how to be friends.

Keeping the visits short will be easier for everyone. This way, when the boys say good-bye, there is a good chance they will be looking forward to the next visit.

You mentioned that your son will have to "prove" to you that he can get along with friends before you'll let him invite someone over again. How can he give you proof if he can't have a friend over? This also implies that your son is at fault. In fact, two children were involved, and you chose to remain uninvolved. Tell your son that both of you will have to try harder to work toward achieving a successful outcome the next time. This is a positive challenge for each of you.

Computer Game Conflicts

Our eight-year-old daughter saved her allowance and worked for months to earn money to buy a computer game. She has spent hours learning how to move through the various levels and has become very skilled. She likes to have friends over so she can show off her skills, and this is creating some bad feelings. When friends get a turn at her game, they lose quickly. Our daughter's turns are long, because she has practiced for hours. Last night she cried because a friend told her she would rather ride her bike after school than sit and watch my daughter play the game. Because the game belongs to my daughter, it doesn't seem right to take it away from her. However, I think in the long run the game will cause more trouble than it's worth.

You need to stop imagining that the game is going to be "more trouble than it's worth." Negative thinking will usually produce negative results. Approach this issue with the attitude that a lot can be learned and your daughter will gain from the experience. Your role is to facilitate this process.

Your daughter demonstrated tenacity in saving the money to buy this game and in practicing for hours to master the game. Such determination can be a major asset throughout her life. Be sure to point this out to her, so she doesn't take her own strengths for granted. She deserves to feel proud of herself!

You are right in thinking that it would be wrong to take the game away. Use this situation to provide a lesson in how to solve problems. Find a time when you and your daughter are calm and discuss the issues that have been presented by the game, assuring her that the two of you are capable of finding constructive ways to handle the situation. Talk about why her friends feel the way they do—they are certainly experiencing frustration and boredom, and perhaps jealousy as well.

Your daughter has several choices. She can try to work out an arrangement with her present friends: in exchange for biking with them, she'll help them become proficient at the game. If they aren't interested, she can try to find friends who are interested in the game and play it only with them; she can still keep her old friends if she puts some time aside for them. Or she may find that she will not be able to mix friends and the game, and she will have to choose between them. If this is the case, you will want to encourage her to maintain her friendships—she can still play the game by herself and sooner or later she'll find someone who will really want to play it with her.

Cruel to New Sister   *We had a happy family of three until our new baby girl arrived. My husband and I deliberately avoid doing things with the baby that will make our three-year-old son jealous. We wait until our son is asleep before we coo over the baby and talk about how terrific she is. When he is awake, we pay much more attention to him than to her. In spite of this, our son still seems aggravated every time he re-members she is around. His hugs turn into suffocating squeezes, and the baby cries. He sweetly rubs her arm for five seconds and then pinches her. We have to punish him for this behavior, but we feel that the punishment will increase his negative feelings. Maybe we should have waited longer to have a second child, but now we are stuck with an upsetting situation.*

It is important for the two of you to deal with reality, rather than fantasy. You will never know if waiting a few years would have made a difference in how your son treated your daughter. Thinking about what might have been can only cause emotional torture. Your job is to figure out why these things are happening and how you can end them.

You might feel better when you realize that the baby isn't your son's only target. Three-year-olds quite typically test limits. Think about how your son be-haves when the baby isn't around. Perhaps you recall his trying to get away with things at the park or the market, and looking to see how you reacted. Our re-actions in these situations teach children a great deal about what is acceptable behavior.

Your son is probably too young to be aware of his own strength, and could unintentionally hurt his sister. Consequently, he needs adult supervision whenever the baby is within his reach.

Perhaps your being overly sensitive to the sibling jealousy has created a problem of its own. Your son does not have the chance to see the natural, loving way you relate to the baby when he isn't there. As parents you are your son's most significant role models. Even though he'll test limits, he needs to observe appropriate ways to interact with a baby. It is okay for children to have feelings of jealousy, so don't try to avoid a perfectly natural emotion.

You mentioned two instances in which your son approached the baby in a gentle way, but then turned harsh. The next time your son's treatment turns harsh stop the encounter immediately. Scoop your son into your arms and praise him for caressing or hugging the baby. You want to reinforce his desirable behavior so that he'll repeat it. If you chastise him for his inappropriate behavior, he will learn that it is a way to get attention; or he may begin to resent the baby. Parents cannot make their children love each other but they can serve as role models of constructive, caring behavior. When children begin to relate to each other in positive ways, the foundation has been laid for their liking and, eventually, loving each other.

My daughter is 15 months old and she loves it when I hold her in the rocking chair and read to her. I used to look forward to this time with her, but during the last few months she has developed the habit of suddenly biting me for no apparent reason. She has enough teeth to make it painful, and my impulse is to slap her. So far I have controlled myself. Somehow, I must make her understand that she cannot bite me. I'm beginning to dread sitting with her.

Biting

Your daughter's sudden attacks create a startle reflex which, quite naturally, prompts you to want to protect yourself. You have been wise to control your impulse to slap her. If we are going to serve as positive role models for our children, we should not respond to one act of physical violence with another.

Young children generally react to loud sounds. Yell "No!" in a loud voice when your daughter bites you, put her down immediately, and hurry to get yourself some ice to avoid swelling. In a firm voice say,

"No biting! You cannot bite people. That really hurts!"
The next time you sit with your daughter, remind her
in a firm tone that she must not bite you. Touch the
area where she last bit you and tell her how much it
hurt. Tell her you know she is not going to do it again.
Every few minutes praise her for controlling her urge
to bite. Continual praise will help her break the habit.

It is not unusual for young children to have a
strong urge to bite, perhaps because of the pressure
on their gums from teething. They need to be taught
that they must not bite people or animals, but there
are things they *can* bite—a pillow or a teething ring,
for example; or they might prefer a small frozen bagel,
which is easy to grasp and soothing to the gums.

**Baby Interferes
with Homework**

*I have girls eight, six, and two years old. My two older
daughters have a lot of homework and they are very serious
about getting good grades. When they come home from
school they have a snack and then go to the room they
share to do their homework. We have a rule that if homework is completely finished they can watch television after
dinner. This has encouraged them to settle down and get
it done in the afternoon.*

*When one of the girls needs help with her work, she
calls me and I go into their room. I can't leave the baby
alone so I take her with me. The problem is that she is old
enough now to cause total chaos in her sisters' room. She
scoots up on chairs and starts pulling things off their desks.
When I tell her to stay off their chairs she heads for their
bookshelves. She is so quick that within seconds she has
emptied the shelves of books, papers, and the little treasures
the girls have carefully displayed there. The girls start
yelling at their sister, I pick her up and angrily tell her
she can't be in their room. The baby starts crying at the
top of her lungs and tries to struggle out of my arms. I
then take her to the other room and feel exhausted. We
can't seem to stop this pattern and my older girls feel upset
because I'm not available to help them understand their
homework. The two-year-old calms down and gets busy*

playing in the other room while I brace myself for the next time the girls call for help.

The typical after-school routine you describe obviously does not work. Before your two-year-old could get around, it was logical to go to your older girls' room to help them, but now it doesn't make sense. Every time you repeat this mistake, you get the same disastrous results. Stop doing it. Tell your older girls to keep their door shut at all times. Explain that someday the little one will be old enough to respect their things, but not yet. If they need help with their homework, tell them to come to you with their materials. Whatever the youngest was doing to occupy herself can just continue while you help with the homework. This should be less disruptive.

Your two-year-old is the "baby" of your family but she isn't really a baby. You need to explain to her what kind of behavior you expect from her. As long as she can successfully manipulate you, she won't take responsibility for her actions. You have shown her that when she tears apart the girls' room she gets a reward—you, in the other room, all to herself. This isn't fair to any of you. Praise her when her behavior is appropriate for a particular situation, especially when you see she is exercising self-control. Give her the chance to be a constructive member of your family and she will undoubtedly live up to your expectations.

CONCLUSION

If we think we know a perfect way to solve a discipline problem, but it doesn't work, it is easy to feel a sense of failure. It is helpful to have several alternative solutions since there is rarely one "right way" to meet a discipline challenge.

It is too easy to fall into the habit of paying undue attention to negative behavior. We then become nags, constantly correcting our children and certainly not helping them to feel good about themselves. We are surprised when even very young children tune us out, ignore what we are saying, or pout and act allergic to us. This rejecting behavior does make sense. As adults, don't we try to avoid people who regularly criticize us? It is a far wiser use of our energy to look for and to reinforce our children's positive actions. If we consistently point out what they are doing that is right, we will help them to feel proud of themselves.

Stressful discipline situations might find us losing our own self-control. We become ineffectual when we contribute to the chaos. The minute we recognize what is happening, we need to slow down, calm down, and let our more mature selves take over. It is worth a few minutes to find a constructive way to approach discipline situations.

Our answers to the following questions will help us meet each discipline challenge in the most effective way we can:

Q. Is this a problem or a challenge?
A. A challenge!

Q. What is the goal of discipline?
A. Self-discipline!

Q. Is discipline for punishment or for change?
A. FOR CHANGE!

Q. Is discipline something we do *to* or *with* children?
A. *With!*

Q. Are we treating our children the way we hope they will treat us and each other?
A. YES!

It might be a good idea to have these questions written on index cards in several different rooms. When you need them, they will be handy to help you move on to a positive discipline path.

Initially, children cannot be left on their own to find solutions to the problems that lead to discipline situations. Children need parents as role models. Parents need to be active participants in helping children to see the issues clearly and to search for constructive solutions. As our children become more adept at this approach, we will do less talking and simply serve as guides for our children's discussions. In time, our children will acquire the communication tools necessary to work through these issues without our help.

What children learn and successfully use during one stage of development may need to be learned in slightly new ways during another stage. Each new phase of development builds on the preceding foundation. With our help, our children will begin to look upon difficult situations as challenges and will view themselves as adept problem-solvers. When problems have been resolved, parents and children feel relieved and want to forget that a conflict ever happened. Later, it is important to review what happened and to congratulate each other over the positive resolution. Remembering these successful interactions could help us find ways for meeting the next discipline challenge. More importantly, as we help our children to recognize and celebrate these successes, we contribute to their feelings of positive self-esteem.

CONCLUSION

No families are completely free of problems. Even families who seem ideally happy face inevitable problems that must be solved. Because there is continual interaction between family members, the complexity of family life may seem overwhelming, but a constructive approach is always possible. Good communication between all members of the family is essential, especially during periods of stress or anger.

A good place to work on family needs is at family discussions or meetings. There have been many references to such meetings throughout this book. Family meetings should not be scheduled more frequently than once a week. Everyone in the family should look forward to them rather than dread them. Plan them for times when no one is likely to be hungry or tired. Parents sometimes make the mistake of using these sessions solely to air complaints about their children—a sure way to make the children resist attending. Family meetings should provide time both to reflect on positive aspects of family life and to mention problems. Planning positive statements about each person in the family can be helpful. Everyone likes to hear that good behavior does not go unnoticed, and everyone likes to receive a compliment. Discuss only essential problems; ignore the insignificant issues. Every family member should be encouraged to be a good listener as well as to make constructive contributions. Even four- and five-year-olds can learn to participate. Obviously, the parents set the atmosphere that determines whether meetings will be successful. Without dominating the discussion, parents can make their children feel that family meetings are a safe place to share thoughts and feelings.

Working together allows family members to see that there is more than one way to solve any particular problem. It can be useful to think of several different solutions for one problem. If one solution does not work, then everyone involved can help choose another. Together, a family can eliminate unwanted habits or change objectionable behavior patterns. Family meetings teach children how to make informed decisions and how to evaluate them. Children also learn that conflicts can be resolved constructively.

Sometimes we take ourselves and each other too seriously. We must remember to have fun together. Smiles and laughter can brighten our spirits and reduce tension. A sense of humor helps put things into perspective and lighten the emotional load. During sorrowful times our families comfort us and during happy times we celebrate each other's victories and accomplishments. Even at the most stressful times, a hug from someone we love can be a big help. Affection between family members can make it easier to cope with the problems of daily living. A physical message cannot be ignored, and a pat or a hug can be more easily understood than words could ever be.

Children add meaning, direction, and purpose to our lives. As we strive to be effective parents, we constantly learn from our children. They continually inspire us to assess our values and priorities. As parents, we can learn to appreciate ourselves and our spouses in new and positive ways, and we can become more competent in every aspect of our lives when we feel competent as parents.

Although being an effective parent is sometimes hard work, we must remember to celebrate the existence of our children and ourselves. As we explore new ways to help our children feel good about themselves, we are fulfilling a primary goal of parents. One of the most rewarding jobs in life is raising a family of decent, healthy, and ultimately useful human beings.

APPENDIXES

APPENDIX I: SEEKING HELP

The basic message of *Guideposts for Growing Up* has been one of faith in the ability of parents and children to resolve their problems and successfully live together. It is important to mention, however, that some issues cannot be easily resolved without outside help. Getting outside help at the right time is critical. It is a mistake to wait until anyone is upset enough to say or do something that will be regretted. Sometimes parents need help because they feel overwhelmed by the demands of raising children. Outside help might also be needed when a child continually sends out warning signals that something is wrong. These signals include nervous habits such as nail biting, constant temper tantrums, extreme moodiness, or withdrawn, depressed behavior. Anything that is totally unusual for your child may be a warning signal and must be given attention.

Obviously, each change in a child's behavior does not require outside help. Your own good judgment will help guide your decisions. Remember that being a parent is difficult and every family faces problems from time to time. If any member of your family seems unusually troubled, do not postpone a discussion with someone who understands children and family dynamics. When parents are receptive to the insights and suggestions presented by an expert, problems can often be resolved effectively.

The types of outside help that are available vary greatly from area to area. Parents have different ideas about what sort of help is acceptable.

Possible resources include pediatricians and family doctors, nurses, psychologists or psychiatrists, members of the clergy, social workers, family or child therapists, teachers, parent-education courses or discussion groups, friends, and relatives. Sometimes, just sharing problems with a good listener can reduce the pressure that parents feel.

APPENDIX II: STAGES IN GROWING UP

This section of *Guideposts for Growing Up* provides a brief overview of growth and development through the first 12 years of life. Most children are advanced for their age in some ways and normal or slower in others. Consequently, even within the same family, the time and way a child passes through each developmental phase is unique. Such factors as genetic makeup, birth order, and environment combine to influence the rate at which a child develops. The material that follows will help you have a better general understanding of what to expect.

BIRTH TO 18 MONTHS

Babies learn to trust their environment and their caretakers when their needs are consistently met. Babies cry to signal hunger, pain, or discomfort, or when they are overly tired. When adults meet their needs with attention and affection, babies begin to feel safe in their world.

Babies need the stimulation of mobiles, music, picture books, colorful objects, sinple toys, and a lot of chatter. (But don't overdo it; they need quiet time, too.) The early months of life are a period of great discovery as babies find their hands, their feet, and other parts of their bodies. They experiment with their own sounds and try to imitate the sounds they hear. Eventually, they can imitate the words of others. Some of the physical milestones of development are sitting, standing, crawling, walking, and throwing things down. As babies begin to move around and discover things to play with, parents are tempted to show them how things work. Resisting the impulse to "teach," allowing children to discover as much as possible on their own, is important for their growth and self-esteem.

Daily routines provide many opportunities for children to take charge of themselves. Usually before their first birthday children will be able to feed themselves. When this happens, parents should present healthy food choices and let the children select what to put into their mouths.

During the first 18 months, it is especially important that children receive encouragement from their parents. They need to feel wanted, appreciated, and loved. This period of a child's life is critical in forming a positive foundation for the future.

EIGHTEEN MONTHS THROUGH TWO YEARS

Children of this age are full of energy, they love to explore and to manipulate objects, and they can entertain themselves for short periods. As their major muscles develop, their walking skills increase. Parents should be patient and offer encouragement as they begin to develop bladder control and, later, control of their bowels.

Children in this age group begin to learn what is acceptable and unacceptable behavior as they test limits. Constant adult supervision is still necessary, because toddlers cannot determine what behavior is safe and what is potentially dangerous. Small children respond well to known routines. Something as minor as a sandwich that is cut in a new way can cause distress. They like being with other children, although they usually play near or with a parent. The children watch each other and often imitate each other, but without interacting. Many toddlers have trouble making choices. They are demanding, often inflexible, and constantly in motion.

Toddlers quickly learn to manipulate their parents through tears and tantrums. Small children are more likely to become upset when they are tired, hungry, or rushed. Often tantrums can be avoided when parents carefully plan routines and are clear about what is acceptable behavior. When parents are overly controlling or critical, however, children can become filled with self-doubt. Although children of this age can be trying, they also can be loving companions—and fun to be with.

THREE-YEAR-OLDS

Three-year-olds begin to show both mental and physical independence. They are proud of their accomplishments and delight in demonstrating them. In many cases, their coordination has developed enough for them to be able to ride tricycles. They can entertain themselves by making simple drawings or playing with blocks. Their communication skills have developed enough for them to tell simple stories or repeat nursery rhymes. They are independent enough to do many care-taking activities, such as using the bathroom, by themselves. With a little assistance, they can dress themselves (although they may have problems with buttons) and they have an easy time getting undressed on their own.

At about three and a half, children may become awkward and, on occasion, stumble and fall. They might develop stuttering or nervous habits, which could be caused by stress or insecurity. Parents should not panic, but try to find the cause of the stress and eliminate it if possible.

Children of this age have fewer temper tantrums because they can do so many things for themselves. Unlike younger children, who use "no" with great frequency, three-year-olds use "yes." They have more patience about having to "wait a few minutes." While toddlers have trouble adapting to sudden changes in plans, three-year-olds like new experiences and are usually willing to try most of the things parents suggest. They are increasingly more social with adults, they learn to share, and they begin to show an interest in peers. They enjoy making up stories and pretending they are real, and they love participating in long sessions of acted-out make-believe.

They express emotional insecurity by crying and whining, and frequently they want parents to reassure them of their love. They often seek this assurance through a paradoxical approach, vehemently saying, "You don't love me." By three and a half, many children are jealous of anyone or anything that takes away the attention of their parents or friends. Three-year-olds often say they want to be just like their parents. They express love through their words and their actions. At this age, or shortly after, children might inform everyone that they are going to grow up and marry their parent of the opposite sex. They need to be told that their plan is impossible, but reassure them that they will have their own special person when they grow up.

Parents can expect their children to inundate them with questions during this period. Children like to give their own answers and then hear what the adult has to say.

A movie, a television show, or something the child hears might cause fears that become greatly inflated at bedtime; the child literally believes that the monsters are out to get him or her, and demand help. When this occurs, it is imperative that the parent be understanding and comfort the child.

It is important that a child of this age learn self-control, how to behave in the company of others, and how to communicate frustrations through words instead of tears and tantrums. Parents need to be patient and set limits. Three-year-olds need to know that their parents have confidence in them, as well as love them.

FOUR- AND FIVE-YEAR-OLDS

Pre-school and kindergarten programs provide an opportunity for children to meet new people and face new challenges. This is a time when children like learning and begin to develop the ability to cooperate with others. By five, most children have learned to play a variety of roles: a follower of older children, a bossy leader of younger children, and a cooperative partner with a peer. Children begin to have strong preferences in playmates and identify with people of their own sex. Their play becomes more complex as their cognitive skills develop. Even though they may invent imaginary friends and make up stories they insist are true, children at this stage begin to understand the difference between the real and the imaginary. They ask detailed questions that require thoughtful answers. They also are curious about their past because hearing about their past helps them feel bigger in the present. At this time, children become more emotionally independent and are frequently more interested in spending time with their peers than with their parents.

Encouraged by their friends, four-year-olds often consciously break rules and behave inappropriately. With or without provocation, they might bite, pinch, hit, or kick; throw or intentionally break things; call people names; or use profanity. They assert their independence by defying parents and teachers. Angry reactions from adults are often met with smirks and a general attitude that communicates "You can't get me." Children often experience mood swings at this stage of development. They begin to understand the concept of "right" and "wrong" but test "wrong" to get adult attention. Parents have to choose when, where, and how to respond. Some things can be ignored but it is imperative to react strongly and firmly to the rest.

Four- and five-year-olds can take care of themselves in their daily routines. They might become fussy about their clothing, and they like others to admire what they are wearing. They enjoy helping around the house, but they usually forget to do the chores they have been assigned. They may be very sloppy about taking care of their clothes and toys and show a disregard for other people's things. Concentration spans lengthen and, by four and a half, many children spend long periods building, painting, or playing dress-up. They like completing what they begin and the uninterrupted time they require should be provided whenever possible.

Fears recede in intensity and begin to shift from fantasy. They may worry about the safety of their parents and the possibility of abandonment. As children move into the fifth year of life, parents often find them to be more emotionally stable; they are more predictable and wild outbursts generally disappear. Almost overnight children of this age become helpful, cooperative, and very responsive to praise. Their defiance evaporates, they want to do things the "right way," and they are extremely sensitive to criticism. Their self-concept is largely drawn from how they think teachers and parents view them. If they haven't been ridiculed or constantly criticized, five-year-olds move through the year developing a sense of purpose, inner control, and direction. The goal is for them to feel comfortable and capable in their world.

FROM SIX TO TWELVE

During this period of growth, children may occasionally demonstrate regressive behavior, such as clinging to a parent, demanding special attention, or throwing temper tantrums. Children of this age are very anxious for peer acceptance and, as a result, try to control their immature behavior at school and in social settings. As a result, parents and siblings are the targets of their frustrations and anger. These children are no longer predominantly influenced by their families; now teachers and peers play a significant role in their lives. The social and academic aspects of school also influence a child's development.

Children at this age begin to learn about and test abstract ideas, such as "being fair" or "being honest." At first, they will often expect other people to adhere to such principles, while they bend rules to accommodate themselves. For example, they might loudly criticize someone caught lying and then, a few minutes later, tell a lie themselves. This testing of principles helps children learn about acceptable behavior and personal responsibility.

Children in the six-to-twelve age range are often described as argumentative, rebellious, oppositional, irritable with their parents—and affectionate and appreciative. Their sudden mood swings are not easy for parents to handle and it is a major challenge to remain calm, understand what is happening, and try to deal with it constructively. Pre-adolescents generally respond well to negotiating as a means of resolving conflicts. Parents who react to misbehavior by letting their children see the logical consequences of their actions help them discover what is fair and why.

A child's fear of failure, at home or at school, can lead to an intense feeling of inferiority and can endanger his or her emotional health. To avoid this, children must be made to feel accepted and loved by their parents, and the parents should refrain from constant criticism. Under these circumstances, even when failures do occur, the children can keep their fragile, emerging self-concept from becoming negative or defeatist.

Six-to-twelve-year-olds are usually on the move, going, doing, trying, seeing; perhaps "restless" best describes them. Because they love being active, they easily miscalculate how dangerous their exploits can be. They become overconfident and, lacking judgment, have accidents.

Nervous reactions such as nail biting, twitches or tics, or finger drumming may suddenly appear. They are usually caused by anxiety and can fade as swiftly as they appear. Parents and teachers can help reduce anxiety by having realistic expectations and goals. Children need adults to praise their efforts, regardless of the outcome. In other words, the effort, as well as the achievement, needs recognition. The environment thus created is one in which young people are willing to take risks as they try to find out who they are.

Children between six and twelve are eager to learn and are interested in a wide variety of things. Generally, they can speak better than they can write, and they like hearing themselves talk. They delight in repeating a story that has gory or scary details. They willfully dominate conversations and may need some help in learning to share the spotlight.

Six-to-twelve-year-olds have a strong desire for peer acceptance. They might participate in sports or join clubs devoted to some special interest and thus begin forming a peer-group identity. They usually like the stability of having a best friend of the same sex. Together, they share secrets, interests, and enemies. They attack their enemies, verbally or physically, without realizing how devastating their words or actions might be. Parents must maintain a delicate balance between interceding and letting the young people work out conflicts on their own.

As children identify with their peers, they want to dress like other members of the group and they sometimes go along with collective decisions, even when they know their parents would disapprove. To pre-adolescents, the admiration and respect of their peers are more important than how their parents or teachers regard their behavior. They might show off, boast, act silly, or even break the law to gain peer approval. They seem to enjoy the shock value of using swear words, belching, and passing gas; and they roar with laughter over their blatant obnoxiousness. They are well aware of what is acceptable and unacceptable and seem to love defying family standards.

On the other hand, pre-adolescents fear rejection by their parents as well as rejection by their friends. This puts parents in a difficult position—they have the responsibility of keeping their children safe, of enforcing family rules, and of maintaining family values without seeming to reject or belittle the children. It is imperative that parents maintain an atmosphere in which the children feel free to discuss their feelings. Their complaints, even when seemingly unjust or ridiculous, should be discussed, not dismissed.

If pre-adolescents are frequently made to feel ashamed of themselves, they may threaten to behave in self-destructive ways. Threats of leaving home or harming themselves are too serious to be taken lightly. When a youngster feels there is no hope, he or she needs professional help. Family therapy can help the child and parents become more effective with each other.

As children pass through these sometimes very trying periods in growing up, parents need to continually believe that there will be a positive outcome. This hope-filled attitude will encourage everyone involved. Undoubtedly there isn't a more challenging job than being a parent; at the same time, there isn't a job with more potential satisfaction and joy.

CONCLUSION

Although it often seems unlikely, children *will* grow up. They'll develop at their own pace and should be accepted and respected for who they are. In such an atmosphere of acceptance and love, they are likely to reach their greatest potential.

INDEX